A-LEVEL YEAR 2 SOCIOLOGY FOR

UNIT 3B (Crime & Deviance)

SOCIOLOGY 3B1 STUDY GUIDE

Published independently by Tinderspark Press
© Jonathan Rowe 2021
www.psychologywizard.net
www.philosophydungeon.weebly.com

CONTENTS

ABOUT THIS BOOK

This book offers advice for teachers and students approaching OCR A-Level Sociology, **Paper 3 Section B1 (Crime & Deviance)**.

Study Guides for **Papers 1** and **2** complete the course.

Paper 3 Section B (Option 1)

This covers about two thirds of **Paper 3** in OCR Sociology. There are 3 questions worth 70 marks out of the 105 marks for the entire paper. It should take candidates 90 minutes to complete.

This is quite a slim study guide for such a big part of the exam!

The reason for this is that the Guide for **1A (Socialisation, Culture & Identity)** has already introduced the foundational concepts that candidates will use throughout the rest of their Sociology A-Level. Some of that material is reiterated here.

Perspectives

Candidates who have completed Study Guide 1A will be familiar with **Functionalism**, **Marxism**, **Feminism** and **Interactionism**. This Guide explores Neo-Marxism in more depth and introduces the **New Right.** In addition, new **Subcultural** and **Realist** Perspectives are introduced that focus Functionalist and Marxist ideas on the problem of crime in modern society.

Functionalism is, strictly speaking, an obsolete theory in Sociology, but its ideas remain very influential in politics and in the media. Even though students who move onto a degree-level study of Sociology at university will find that Functionalism barely features, it is presented here as a theoretical perspective that is both intellectually and morally equivalent to the 'conflict' perspectives of Marxism and Feminism. The aim is to help students evaluate sociological arguments from any point of view.

Studies

Sociological 'studies' (for A-Level purposes) are often papers published in academic journals, but are sometimes magazine articles, pamphlets produced by charities or activists or popular books.

Where texts are particularly famous or influential, I offer their names, but candidates are not expected to know the names of studies in the exam. All the studies referenced in this Study Guide are brought together at the end in a revision aid (p90).

CRIME & DEVIANCE: CONTENT

What's this topic about?

This introduces you to the main sociological theories about Crime, in particular why crime occurs, what can be done about it and how it should be defined and measured.

This should help you answer some important questions:

- What is Crime in society: is it a terrible threat to the social order, a necessary evil or something that has been exaggerated to demonise certain unpopular social groups?

- Why is there Crime and Deviance: is it natural for people to break the rules or are they driven to do it by problems in society itself?

- What should be done about Crime: are criminals misunderstood and in need of help and rehabilitation? or are they dangers to society who need to be punished and locked away? Can we reduce crime by monitoring everybody closely or do we need instead to build a fairer society where crime isn't necessary?

Deviance

Deviance is behaviour that goes against social **norms**, leading to reactions like shock, outrage, disgust or fear. People feel strongly about deviance and deviant people are often condemned, tormented and outcast. However, deviance varies from culture to culture and time to time. This suggests it is, at least to some extent, **socially constructed** (p12). Deviant behaviour can involve taking drugs, dressing inappropriately, using forbidden language or disrespecting people or institutions that society considers important.

A lot of behaviour that used to be considered deviant is fairly normative now. For example, homosexuality, drug taking and wearing casual/revealing clothes used to be viewed very negatively but attitudes are changing. Deviance tends to bring on **informal social control**.

Crime is behaviour that goes against the written laws of the country and carries **formal sanctions**. It is a subject of **formal social control**. A lot of laws involve property, such as theft and trespass and vandalism. Laws are always being created and abolished and they also vary between countries and times. Homosexuality used to be illegal as did being a witch, but those things are no longer crimes in Western countries.

Many things are both criminal *and* deviant, such as murder and rape. Some things are *criminal but not particularly deviant*: the law will punish you for speeding or parking where you shouldn't, but your friends and workmates won't think worse of you for it. Other things are *deviant but not criminal*: it causes shock and outrage when someone cheats on their husband or wife but in Western countries the police won't get involved (even if the cheated person wishes they would).

CHAPTER ONE – MEASURING CRIME & DEVIANCE

This first part of the course is called '*How are crime and deviance defined and measured?*' so the first task is to think about some definitions. This is done through the broad Perspectives of Consensus, Conflict and Social Action introduced earlier in the A-Level.

SOCIAL ORDER & CONTROL

Social control is the way that society gets people to conform. This is done through the **agencies of social control** covered **in 1A: Socialisation, Culture & Identity**. These agencies can be **formal** (like the police and the courts) or **informal** (like families and peer groups).

Social order refers to the organisation of society around its beliefs: who holds power, who gets to define what is normal and what is deviant, what the formal agencies of social control are and what power they have, what happens to the deviants who break the rules?

The philosopher **Thomas Hobbes (1651)** answers this by describing a **social contract**. The contract is a metaphor (nobody literally signs a contract) for the sort of 'deal' we enter into with society: we give up certain freedoms to do as we please and in return society protects us and gives us the opportunity to study, earn and spend money and enjoy culture.

Consensus View of Social Order & Control

Émile Durkheim (1893) claims social order is based on shared values. It's a 'ground up' view that people naturally generate social order from their daily interactions – from their **culture**. This creates **social solidarity** which is a feeling of belonging. The people brought together by this experience a **collective conscience** – a shared sense of right and wrong and the meaning of life.

Durkheim contrasts **'mechanical solidarity'** of traditional pre-modern societies with the **'organic solidarity'** of modern societies. Mechanical solidarity exists when everybody does the same work (farming or hunting). Organic solidarity is when everybody is different from their neighbour (doing different jobs, different religions, etc) but they are all **interdependent**: they rely on each other to fulfil different roles and functions like different organs in the body.

This is a **Functionalist** view (p47). It proposes that the police act on our behalf and exert social control with our consent. Criminals break the social solidarity of the community and they need to be stopped and brought back into line to preserve social order. Social control is an expression of the community's values: our disapproval of crime and outrage at deviancy.

Conflict View of Social Order & Control

Karl Marx (1858) argues that social order is based on the economic structure of society. Marx argued that that there are two components to society: the **base** (resources and the technology to exploit them) and the **superstructure** (all the institutions like government, churches, schools and families).

Marx argues that the superstructure grows out of the base and reflects the values of the **ruling class** that controls the base. The superstructure justifies the power of the ruling class. The base and the superstructure create and maintain social order together.

In **Capitalism**, this leads to a tiny ruling class dominating a huge working class. Social order is all about keeping this arrangement going and social control is used to stop anyone from threatening this arrangement.

This is a **Marxist** view (p53) but a similar argument is made by **Feminists** (p58), that social order consists of making half the population (women) subordinate to the other half and social control is used to keep women in line by justifying the inequality – or by threats and violence when women don't conform.

This view proposes that the police are acting on behalf of the ruling class in society. Criminals are threatening the wealth and power of the ruling group and they need to be stopped and brought back into line. Punishments are an expression of the **ruling class ideology**, and the fear of crime makes people consent to social control even though it isn't in their interests.

Social Action View of Social Order & Control

The Consensus and Conflict Perspectives are both **structuralist** views: neither of them recognises that individuals have agency or input into how society works and they propose that big institutions or impersonal economic forces are really in charge. They are **macro perspectives** viewing things on a society-wide scale.

Max Weber (1922) developed an **Interactionist** (p59) and **micro perspective**, which takes into account individual agency as well as powerful institutions. It is called a Social Action Perspective because it takes into account how society controls us but also how we can act to influence society.

Weber thinks **social actions** are of four types:

- **Traditional:** this involves following laws and customs because 'that's how it's always been done' and a lot of social order comes from this; it is similar to the Consensus and Conflict Perspectives
- **Affective:** this involves acting on feelings without thinking; both Consensus and Conflict Perspectives underestimate emotions
- **Value-Rational:** this is acting on your conscious beliefs, often the result of socialisation (e.g. believing in a religion); Consensus sees this as healthy for society but Conflict sees it as ruling class ideology at work
- **Instrumental-Rational:** acting deliberately in order to bring about changes in society; this is something Consensus and Conflict both underestimate

This view proposes that social order is shaped by traditions or powerful institutions (as Durkheim would agree) and these institutions support the wealthy and the powerful (as Marx would agree) – but ordinary people exert influence and can shape the way they are policed and controlled.

AO2 ILLUSTRATION: BLACK LIVES MATTER

Black Lives Matter (BLM) is a protest movement that started in 2012 when a Black high school student **Trayvon Martin** was shot and killed by an armed neighbourhood watchman who was later found not guilty of murder. In 2013, #BLM became a popular hashtag for online activism (*c.f.* **3A: Globalisation & the Digital Social World**). In 2014, the shooting of another Black American, **Michael Brown**, triggered weeks of protests against police violence in Ferguson, Missouri. More recently, the murder of **George Floyd** by a White police officer in 2020 prompted worldwide protests against racism and police brutality.

The BLM movement is de-centralised with no formal leadership or structure. A lot of activists speaking under the BLM banner call for defunding the police but also for feminism and LGBT rights, immigration reform and Social Justice.

In 2016, American football player **Colin Kaepernick 'took the knee'** instead of standing for the National Anthem, as a protest against racism and police brutality. The gesture has been widely adopted outside of sports, especially by the BLM movement.

Functionalists tend to defend the police by claiming they use proportionate force in a dangerous job (they take National Anthems quite seriously too). From a **Conflict Perspective**, the police serve the interests of the (White) ruling class and oppressing Black working class people is part of how they maintain social order. However, a **Social Action** Perspective shows how a **party** (the BLM movement) and individuals with **status** (Colin Kaepernick) can win public support and possibly bring about a change in social order and control.

Research: the Black Lives Matter movement and debates about 'taking the knee'

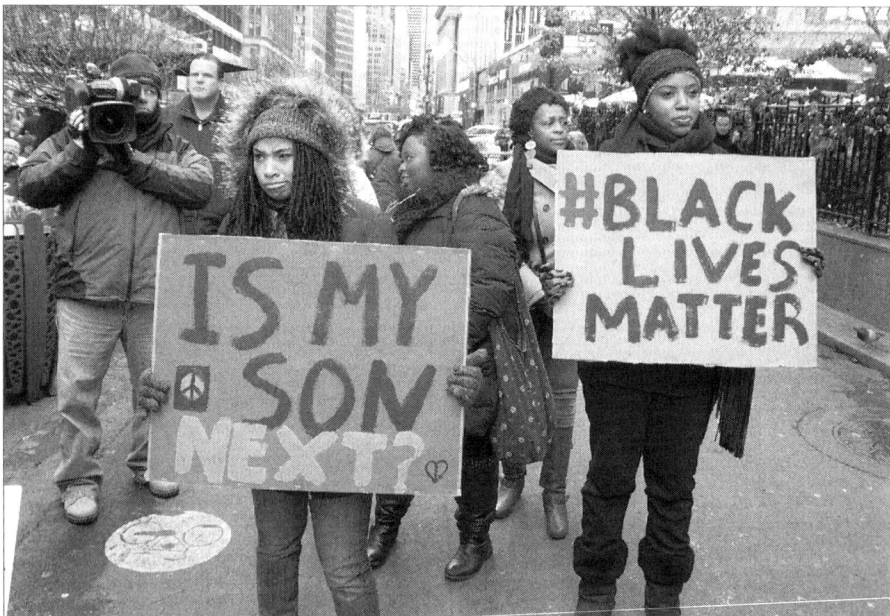

THE RELATIVITY OF CRIME & DEVIANCE

Crime and deviance are relative concepts. That means that what is defined as criminal or deviant is relative to the society where it happens or the Identity of the person doing it. Or to put it plainly, there's no absolute definition of what is or what isn't a crime or a deviant act and societies as well as onlookers make different distinctions.

For example, in Muslim-majority countries, drinking alcohol might be considered deviant or actually illegal. Gun ownership is legal in the USA but the exact laws regarding what guns can be owned and carried in public varies from State to State. As noted in **1A: Socialisation, Culture & Identity**, the age of majority (the age at which young people are considered adults) varies from country to country, so it's legal to sell alcohol to a 18-year-old in the UK but this is a crime in the USA. The rights of women, their access to education and what they can wear in public without being criticised or even arrested varies from country to country.

There is also **selective policing** where people from marginalised backgrounds are more likely to be viewed as 'acting suspiciously' and classed as committing a crime.

Consensus View of Relativity

The Consensus Perspective sees social order arising out of culture, so where cultures differ around the world you would expect the definitions of crime and deviance to vary too. However, alongside the variation, there's a lot of consistency too. Societies vary in how they punish crimes like murder and the things that might justify killing someone (such a defending your home or your family's honour) but they all have a crime called 'murder.'

Functionalists claim that culture ultimately reflects human biology: we are animals with physiological needs. **Talcott Parsons (1951)** argues there are functional prerequisites that a society has to meet in order for people to flourish. These include **adaptation to the environment** (providing people with food and shelter) and **pattern maintenance** (educating the next generation and passing on culture to them).

This means there are limits to how wildly societies can differ from each other. A society that bans having children or that makes it illegal to sell food will soon die out (and only the lawbreakers will survive).

Functionalists often believe that Western democracies with a Capitalist economy are the most advanced and successful because they best reflect our biological needs. This is the **'March of Progress.'** This belief leads to the idea that Western ideas of crime and deviance – especially the concept of human rights – should be exported to other countries so they can benefit from them too. As human rights become accepted round the world, crime and deviance become less relative – they are judged by a universal standard.

Research: revisit your notes on Globalisation and Cultural Homogenisation from **3A: Globalisation & the Digital Social World**; the exporting of human rights is another aspect of Global Culture

Conflict View of Relativity

The Conflict Perspective sees social order being imposed to suit the interests of a ruling class. Different societies around the world will have a different economic base (some will be industrialised, some agricultural, some rich in oil or rare minerals) and this means their superstructure of institutions and culture will develop differently. This explains a lot of variation in ideas about crime and deviance.

Some societies might not have a Capitalist system in place and so don't have a tiny ruling class exploiting everyone else. This would lead to very different ideas about crime and deviance.

However, Capitalism has gone global. This means that **Marxists** end up agreeing with Functionalists that societies don't vary too much, although for different reasons.

Marxists are interested in **selective policing**. The power of ruling class ideology means that bystanders are more likely to report the behaviour of people who are working class or Black as 'suspicious' and the police are more likely to arrest (or, in the USA, shoot) suspects from marginalised groups.

Feminists similarly think that Patriarchy is a worldwide problem. Different societies are relatively safe or relatively dangerous for women, but they all subordinate women to men in some sense. Violence against women is a worldwide problem and one which all societies tend to ignore or justify. Moreover, Feminists accuse the police of not taking violence against women as seriously as violence against other men.

Research: revisit your notes on the 'transnational bourgeoisie' from **3A: Globalisation & the Digital Social World** and link crime and deviance to a **Networked Global Society**.

Social Action View of Relativity

Differing definitions of crime and deviance are easily explained by the Social Action Perspective, which recognises that ordinary people – especially when united by a movement and emboldened by strong beliefs – can reshape the society around them.

Max Weber (1905) links the invention of Capitalism itself to the '*Protestant work ethic*.' He proposes that a group of European Christians (Protestants) developed a belief that God commanded hard work and unselfishness but revealed his blessing through success in business. This motivated people to work hard to earn money, but instead of spending the money on luxuries or religious monuments they re-invested the profits back into their businesses.

Weber's point is that a relatively small number of people can reshape society in unexpected ways if they have strong beliefs. This is similar to the Marxist view that the spread of Capitalism will create similarities in crime and deviance everywhere, but Social Action claims different societies will have different reactions to Capitalism, based on their beliefs. Beliefs also affect how police deal with crime, especially why some people are targeted by the police with greater force.

AO2 ILLUSTRATION: BLACK LIVES MATTER continued

The **Black Lives Matter** movement was prompted by the killings of Black Americans by the police – and specifically White police officers. Here are some tragic examples:

17-year-old **Trayvon Martin** was shot in 2012 by a White neighbourhood watch volunteer armed with a 9mm semi-automatic pistol. The killer was arrested but acquitted, because it could not be proved he hadn't been acting in self-defence.

In 2014, **Michael Brown** (18) was walking with a friend when they were stopped by a police officer. The officer shot and killed Brown but claimed self-defence and was not charged.

In 2018, **Stephon Clark** (22) was shot more than 20 times while standing in his grandmother's yard. They believed he was holding a gun but it was a mobile phone. No officers were charged with his death.

In 2020, **Breona Taylor** (26) and her boyfriend were asleep when plainclothes police officers broke into their house looking for drugs. Shots were fired and Taylor was killed. None of the officers were charged for Taylor's death.

Also in 2020, **George Floyd** was arrested walking home from a convenience store. The police officer Derek Chauvin knelt on Floyd's neck for 9 minutes 26 seconds, despite Floyd repeatedly telling officers he could not breathe before he died. The incident was filmed by bystanders. Chauvin was convicted of murder.

Black Lives Matter claim that Black Americans are stopped more often than White citizens and are more likely to be killed by police violence. This illustrates **relativity** because the same behaviour carried out by a White or a Black person gets different responses from the police, with the Black person more likely to be challenged and dealt with violently.

Black Lives Matter – We Won't Be Silenced (photo: alisdare21)

SOCIAL CONSTRUCTION OF CRIME & DEVIANCE

Social construction is the way that human interpretations shaped by cultural and historical contexts create characteristic that are typically thought to be objective and biological—such as gender, race, class and sexuality (**Subramaniam, 2010**).

All sociologists are 'soft' social contructivists, because they admit that social attitudes play a part in shaping what counts as a crime or a deviant act – this is the basis for the **relativism of crime and deviance**.

Some sociologists are 'hard' social constructivists who go further than this and argue that criminal and deviant acts are *entirely* a product of social attitudes: society creates crime and crime wouldn't exist if it wasn't for social attitudes.

Consensus View of Social Construction

Functionalists assume that biology shapes society to some extent. This means they think that crime is inevitable, given that we are competitive animals and there will never be a perfect match between the culture we create and our biological limitations.

Émile Durkheim (1895) explains this by imagining the **'society of saints'** where everyone is an "*exemplary individual*" and "*crimes are unknown.*" Durkheim argues that there will still be "*faults*" among the saints. These faults appear trivial to outsiders (perhaps, forgetting to say 'Bless You' when someone sneezes) but among the saints they cause "*the same scandal that the ordinary offense does in ordinary consciousness.*" This illustrates both the **relativity** of deviance and the way it is **socially constructed**.

Despite this, Functionalists believe crime is real: criminal activities actually happen and are not entirely in the imagination of newspapers and governments. This understanding informs the **Right Realist** Perspective (p51).

Conflict View of Social Construction

Traditional **Marxists** tend towards 'hard' social constructivism when it comes to crime. They propose that most crime is really a fiction created by police reports, government statistics and news stories to demonise marginalised groups (especially the working class) and spread fear. The Capitalist class is then able to justify heavy-handed policing to deal with a non-existent problem. Meanwhile **white collar crime** is barely reported or policed.

The story of Marxist criminology is one of gradually surrendering this position in favour of a 'soft' constructivist one. **Neo-Marxists** in the 1970s admit that working class crime exists (p54) and **Left Realism** in the 1980s and '90s acknowledges the need to be tough on crime as well as the causes of crime (p56).

Feminists identify the opposite problem: crimes against women are downplayed rather than exaggerated and it's common to 'blame the victim' for the way she acted or dressed. This 'soft' social construction of crimes against women makes women responsible for their own victimisation and justifies male criminals for acting out of 'provocation' or a 'misunderstanding.'

Social Action View of Social Construction

The Social Action Perspective promotes the concept of 'hard' Social Construction. **Howard Becker** developed a type of Interactionism called **Labelling Theory** in his book *Outsiders* **(1963)**. Becker suggests that our interactions with others causes us to pick up 'labels' that affect how other people view us and therefore how future interactions work out. Some people are given **deviant labels** (e.g. 'thief' or 'promiscuous'). Over time, we can **internalise** labels and believe they are part of our Identity: this is the **Self-Fulfilling Prophecy (SFP)**. Some labels have **Master Status** and overrule all other labels.

Becker defines the process like this: *"social groups create deviance by making rules whose infraction creates deviance, and by applying those rules to particular people and labelling them as outsiders."*

This means that society interprets the behaviour of people with the 'deviant' label as deviant, even if it is entirely innocent (and, indeed, no different from other behaviour going on all around) – and interprets the behaviour of 'respectable' people as non-deviant even when they behave in exactly the same way.

If you remember being punished by a teacher for something the rest of the class was doing too you will have a lot of sympathy with this theory.

AO2 ILLUSTRATION: SLUTWALKS

In 2011, a Canadian police officer suggested *"women should avoid dressing like sluts"* if they want to avoid sexual assault. There was a Feminist outcry against this type of victim-blaming. The protest took the form of a **SlutWalk**, a march where women dressed in a way considered to be 'slutty' such as short skirts, stockings and scanty tops, asserting their freedom to dress how they wish and right to be protected by the law when so doing. The organisers expected 200 people to take part in Toronto but 3000 participated.

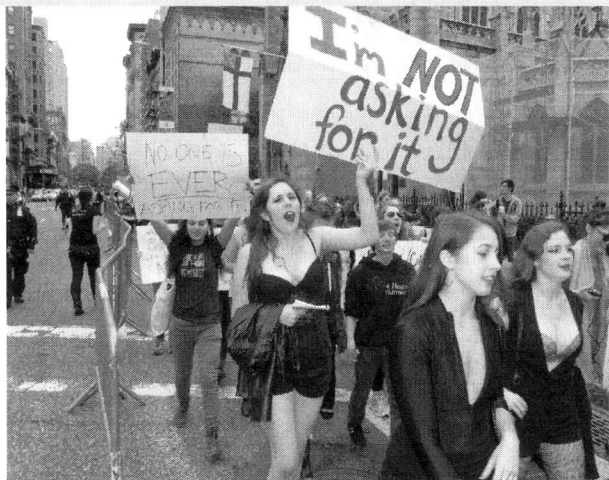

SlutWalk NYC October 2011 (photo: David_shankbone)

Similar SlutWalks have taken place in cities worldwide. Feminist **Jessica Valenti (2011)** says: *"SlutWalks have become the most successful feminist action of the past 20 years."*

SlutWalks are also part of the #MeToo movement and **4th Wave Feminism**, in particular its **sex-positive** attitude (*c.f.* **3A: Globalisation & the Digital Social World**). They draw attention to the **socially constructed** nature of sexual crimes against women, since women's clothing is viewed as provoking (and excusing) assaults. They also point out the **relativism of crime**, since assaults against men are not treated less seriously based on how men are dressed. According to **Valenti (2011)**: *"The idea that women's clothing has some bearing on whether they will be raped is a dangerous myth feminists have tried to debunk for decades."*

RESEARCH PROFILE: PEARSON (1983)

Geoffrey Pearson wrote *Hooligan: A history of respectable fears* **(1983)** after observing reactions to the riots in Brixton (London) and other British cities. Pearson noted the way Right Wing commentators blamed poorly socialised youths and single parent families for the riots and wrote this book as a response.

*The attitudes Pearson is addressing are those of the **New Right**, which emerged at this time.*

Pearson shows how concerns about aimless and violent youths are nothing new. He gives a detailed analysis of the **Teddy Boy Subculture** of the 1950s, which shocked post-War Britain with gang fighting and vandalism. He reports how punishments were toughened up to deal with these delinquents, including the first **'short sharp shock'** Detention Centres (p68) and the Youth Training Scheme to get school-leavers into jobs (similar to later views by the **New Right**, p50).

Pearson shows that the 'Teds' appeared before televisions were widely owned, rock & roll music had crossed over from America or wartime meat rationing had ended, so they were not the result of bad influences from TV, America or having too much comfort.

Instead, Pearson shows that these youth gangs were nothing new and British society has *always* had these fears about delinquency. He compares the Teds to the original Edwardian delinquents known as 'Muggers' or 'Hooligans' and details the fighting, street crime and assaults on police from the hot summer of 1868. A generation earlier, the 'Garrotters' of caused concern in Victorian Britain and the trend goes back to the 'unruly apprentices' of the Middle Ages.

Pearson's point is that youth deviance and crime has always been with us but is often presented as something new and used to justify a crackdown on working class people and criticism of their families and lifestyles. This is a **Marxist** view that shows that apparent crime waves can be **socially constructed** and only **relative** to other periods in history. However, it also resembles **Durkheim**'s argument that crime and deviance are inevitable (p12).

Research: if you studied Youth Deviance and Moral Panics for **1B: Youth Subcultures** then Pearson's work makes an excellent study for those topics too.

MEASURING CRIME & DEVIANCE: A TOOLKIT

It is important to measure crime in order to identify trends: is a particular type of crime becoming more common or less common? It's essential to know this to work out how to deploy police resources and to calculate whether crime prevention strategies are working.

The Dark Figure

Clive Hollin (1989) points out a major problem with criminology which he calls '**the Dark Figure of unrecorded crime**.' This is the idea that most crime goes unrecorded – Hollin suggests only 25% of crime makes it into the recorded figures.

The Dark Figure is partly a result of crimes being reported but not recorded (e.g. because the police don't take them seriously). It includes victims who don't report crime out of shame or fear of reprisals or a distrust of the police. Some crimes are reported to other agencies (like insurance companies or schoolteachers) and dealt with at that level, without involving the law. There are crimes that people don't realise have happened to them, such as fraud. Sexual assaults can fall into this category if the victims blame themselves and don't view the attack as a crime.

Finally, there are so-called 'victimless' crimes that target business (like shoplifting) or other institutions (like tax evasion) and this includes crimes against the environment. Of course, there *are* victims of 'victimless' crimes (such as health problems from pollution or injuries from safety standards being ignored) but nobody feels *personally* targeted by them so there isn't a strong motive to report or investigate them.

RESEARCH PROFILE: MUMSNET (2012)

The social media site *Mumsnet* carried out a **Sexual Assault Survey** of 1609 users as part of their '*We Believe You*' campaign in 2012: 27% reported being raped and 52% sexually assaulted but 83% of those who experienced rape or sexual assault did *not* report it to the police, with one half saying this was because of shame and two thirds saying they would hesitate to report rape or sexual assault because they didn't expect their attacker to be convicted.

Mumsnet founder **Justine Roberts** blames "*the feeling among many women that they can't talk about these crimes for fear of being treated unsympathetically, denying them access to practical and emotional support when they need it most.*"

This is a **victim survey** (p18) with a **volunteer (self-selecting) sample**, so it's possible the results are influenced by respondents who had a bad experience of the justice system (and want to complain) but those who had a good experience (and who reported the crime) did not feel the need to respond to the survey.

Research: find out more about the 'We Believe You' survey; review your notes from **2A: Research Methods** on volunteer sampling

OFFICIAL CRIME STATISTICS (OCS)

Official crime statistics (OCS) are records kept by the government. They are used to track the rise and fall of crime nationally and regionally and are the figures that tend to get reported in the news. These statistics are collected every 6 months by the Home Office and published by the **Office for National Statistics (ONS)**.

Positive Views of Official Crime Statistics

Official statistics are quite up to date, cover the whole country and provide a **'whole count'** – they are not an estimate based on a sample. They consist of **quantitative data** which can be analysed statistically to get objective conclusions about **patterns and trends** in crime (p24).

These statistics are **standardised**, which means the different categories have a fixed meaning and relate to legal distinctions (e.g. different classes of illegal drugs). This standardisation means you can trace the statistics back over many years and detect the rise and fall of different types of crimes. This is essential for investigating whether **crime prevention strategies** are working (p63) and how crime rates relate to other changes in society (like unemployment increasing or decreasing) which is important for **explaining crime** (p45).

Negative Views of Official Crime Statistics

OCS suffers particularly badly from the **Dark Figure** of unrecorded crime because many people do not report crimes to the authorities. Some crimes are reported but to authorities other than the government: children might report a crime to parents or schoolteachers who deal with it without involving the police. Criminals tend to deal with crime themselves (leading to gang warfare) rather than involving the authorities. **Summary offences** (like motoring offences) don't get included in the figures. These gaps in the data make OCS **invalid**.

Although OCS are standardised, the categories used often change. Sometimes this is because the law changes (for example, a previously legal drug is criminalised, creating a lot more crimes when people continue using it) or categories are re-defined. This means it's not always possible to draw clear trends over time and it makes OCS **unreliable**.

Some crimes are reported more if a campaign has drawn public attention to the problem: this creates the false impression that the crime has become more common when it is merely being reported more often. This makes the data **invalid** and **unreliable**.

*If you studied **Moral Panics** for 1B (options in **Youth Subcultures** or **Media**), you can apply your understanding of **deviancy amplification spirals** to this problem with OCS.*

OCS figures are quite simplistic. They do not gather rich data on the identity of the victim or the motives of the criminal – for that, you need a **victim survey** (p18) or a **self-report study** (p20).

AO2 ILLUSTRATION: CRIMES KNOWN TO THE POLICE (CKP)

There are 43 police forces in England & Wales, along with the British Transport Police and separate police forces in Scotland and Northern Ireland. Each police force keeps a record of reported crimes and submits this to the Home Office every 6 month to form a major part of OCS.

According to **John Lambert (1970)**, the problem with CKP lies in **police discretion**. Police officers have choice (discretion) over whether to arrest someone, issue a caution or a more informal warning. Warnings often aren't recorded and police discretion extends to what particular offence to arrest or caution someone for and what details to put in the final written report. This can make CKP a very **unreliable** measure of crime and particularly prone to **labelling** (pX), since the police often act with the concept of an **'ideal criminal'** in mind and are more likely to record as crimes behaviour by people meeting this **stereotype**.

This flaw with CKP is used to explain the over-representation of ethnic minorities (p34) in OCS.

Police forces are given political direction by the Home Office, which can include instructions to focus on particular crimes and focus less on others (for example, to concentrate on knife crimes but not on burglaries). This also skews CKP, showing an increase in some crimes and a decrease in others that isn't based on reality (**invalid**). **Feminists** accuse the police of not taking crimes against women seriously and being hostile and unbelieving when women report rape, leading to lower recording of these crimes.

Research: find out more about police discretion in the debate over 'Stop & Search'

RESEARCH PROFILE: HOLDAWAY (1980)

Simon Holdaway is a pioneer of police research. While he was a sergeant in the London Metropolitan Police in the 1970s, Holdaway conducted a ground-breaking (**covert**) ethnographic study of police work: *The Occupational Culture of Urban Policing*.

Holdaway argues that the police cannot deal with all offences so they have to prioritise. This leads to an **occupational culture** (like a **subculture**) which **socialises** officers into a set of unusual norms and values. **Police discretion** is at the centre of this culture and means 'turning a blind eye' when an offence is too minor or not worth the effort to follow up. The occupational culture values action and aggression, which leads to norms focusing on particular types of offences (e.g. violent crime) at the expense of less exciting crimes (e.g. traffic offences, shoplifting).

Holdaway also reports a culture of racism revealed by derogatory language, jokes and banter between White police officers in police stations.

Since it is based on his own experiences as well as interviews and observations with ordinary police officers, Holdaway's study carries a lot of authority (**validity**). However, policing has changed a lot since then, notably the Metropolitan Police being criticised by the **Macpherson Report** (p57) which led to an attempt to change the occupational culture.

VICTIM SURVEYS

Victim Surveys involve asking members of the public what crimes they have been a victim of in the past.

Positive Views of Victim Surveys

Victim surveys reveal the sort of crimes that people do not report to the police (or feel were ignored by the police), so they are very important for exploring the **Dark Figure** of unrecorded crime (p15).

Victim surveys also reveal **patterns of victimisation** that does not show up in police reports. For example, official statistics tend to show that women are unlikely to be victims of crime, but victim surveys allow women to report many more experiences of victimisation that they either do not report to the police or feel are not taken seriously by the police.

Like OCS, victim surveys are carried out on a **national level** but **local surveys** are also conducted, which shows the effect of crime at a neighbourhood level. They can be **standardised** just like OCS but they can gather more supplementary data than OCS, such as the victim's age, class, gender or ethnicity and their feelings of safety or trauma.

Negative Views of Victim Surveys

Victim surveys do not provide a 'whole count' – they are a **sample** of the total population and trends can only be **estimated** based on them. If the sample is unrepresentative then the data will be **unreliable**.

Many people approached to take part in a victim survey do not respond and it is possible that these are people with no experience of crime, meaning that the data is skewed to exaggerate victimisation. Some people are not included in victim surveys, such as people with no fixed address (homeless, migrants, etc) and children.

Since the survey is a written questionnaire, people with low levels of literacy might be intimidated by it and if they refuse to complete it (or complete it badly) then the results will not reflect their experiences. This tends to mean that victim surveys reflect the experiences of better-educated and more middle-class people.

There is also the possibility that victim surveys are answered untruthfully. Respondents might be too ashamed or traumatised to write about a crime. Alternatively, they might **exaggerate** the seriousness or frequency of crime in their life (perhaps in the hope that politicians will act on the results or simply because they have vivid imaginations).

Victim surveys do not gather data on 'victimless' crimes (such as shoplifting), crimes that are not detected by the victim (such as fraud) or crimes the victim doesn't interpret as crime (such as some sexual assaults).

AO2 ILLUSTRATION: CRIME SURVEY FOR ENGLAND & WALES

The British Crime Survey (BCS) began in 1982. After the Scottish Government introduced its own survey, the BCS became the **Crime Survey for England & Wales (CSEW)** in 2012.

The CSEW surveys 50,000 people aged 16+ every year but also conducts 4000 interviews with children aged 10-15. The results are published alongside CKP by the Office for National Statistics (ONS). It measures experiences of crime in the previous 12 months. The response rate is only 75%, which lowers the reliability of the data, especially if people with very high or very low experiences of crime are not responding. However, this is still quite a high response rate relative to many other surveys.

The CSEW **caps** the number of times a crime can be reported at 5. In other words, if you were mugged 7 times in the last year, this would be treated as 5 muggings. **Graham Farrell (2007)** estimates that the CSEW underestimates crime by 3 million offences a year because of this and this might particularly affect the reporting of domestic violence, which could be 140% higher. This cap has been **standardised** since the start of the BCS, so trends are **reliable** over time.

Research: visit the CSEW website on https://ukdataservice.ac.uk/

RESEARCH PROFILE: JONES, MACLEAN & YOUNG (1986)

A local victim survey that is very important in the history of sociology is the **Islington Crime Survey**, carried out by a research team from Middlesex University: **Trevor Jones**, **Brian Maclean** & **Jock Young**.

*If you recognise **Jock Young** as a famous **Neo-Marxist** sociologist, well done!*

Islington is a borough in North London that has always had high levels of deprivation. The team surveyed 2000 residents about their experience of crime (which was rising sharply at the time), their fear of crime and their attitudes to the police. Instead of just using a questionnaire, they carried out sympathetic unstructured interviews.

A third of respondents had experienced serious crime in the previous twelve months, such as sexual assault, domestic violence and racial attacks. A quarter avoided going out after dark because of fear of crime and 28% felt unsafe in their own homes. Women experienced a 'curfew' – over half the women in the sample never went out after dark because of their fear of crime.

These results were (and are) shocking. They caused Jones et al. to re-assess their **Radical Criminology** (p54) views and develop a new **Left Realist** position (p56) based on the insight that crime is real and the poorest people are the victims.

The use of **unstructured interviews** lowers the **reliability** of the study, even though it increases the willingness of the respondents to open up (**high validity**). A local survey like this cannot be generalised to other areas or to Islington today, over 30 years later.

SELF-REPORT STUDIES

Victim studies question the victims of crimes, but **self-report studies** question the criminals themselves. The simplest form of self-report study involves a questionnaire with a list of offences and the respondents tick off the offences they have committed (either ever committed or committed in the last year).

They're a bit like those 'Never Have I Ever …?' memes that circulate online.

NEVER HAVE I EVER

GIVE YOURSELF 1 POINT FOR EACH THING YOU HAVEN'T DONE

1. Skipped school
2. Broken a bone
3. Fired a gun
4. Done drugs
5. Been in a limo
6. Gotten a tattoo
7. Ridden a horse
8. Sung karaoke
9. Gotten a ticket
10. Been arrested
11. Gone zip lining
12. Been on TV
13. Been on a cruise
14. Gotten a peircing
15. Smoked
16. Met a celeb
17. Been skydiving
18. Had a 1 night stand
19. Skinny dipped
20. Been drunk

This one went viral on Twitter in 2020

Positive Views of Self-Report Studies

Self-report studies are an effective way to explore the **Dark Figure** of unrecorded crime (p15), because the offenders know what they have done, even if they got away with it undetected. They often challenge stereotypes about the **'ideal criminal'** since they often reveal the extent of female criminality and middle-class criminality to be much higher than OCS suggest.

Self-report studies are often **longitudinal**, getting the same cohort to repeat the questionnaire every year. This provides valuable data about how criminal behaviour changes with age or in response to changes in the law or new policing strategies.

Negative Views of Self-Report Studies

There are huge problems with getting people to self-report the crimes they have committed. People who have committed serious crimes will not confess to them on a questionnaire. Even if they did, this would create an **ethical problem** for the researchers, who would then have to report the crime to the police or else become 'accessories after the fact' (because they are helping to conceal a crime).

Because of this, most self-report studies are of teenager cohorts and focus on **delinquency** and minor crimes. However, these are a type of offending that is often missed out by OCS since many people don't think it's worth reporting and police often respond with informal warnings.

AO2 ILLUSTRATION: SELECTIVE POLICING

One of the main findings to come out of self-report surveys is that the stereotype of the 'ideal criminal' might not be based in reality. Various self-report studies suggest that 50-90% of the population admit to behaviour which could get them arrested.

In particular, the difference in offences reported by working-class and middle-class people isn't as great as is thought (**Martin Gold, 1966**, found it a working-class-to-middle-class ratio of 1.5:1) and the offending of women is closer to men that is assumed (**Anne Campbell, 1981**, found a male-to-female ratio of 1.3:1). However, both of these were self-report studies of delinquents, not adult criminals.

Steven Box (1983) suggests that this data indicates the flaws in a **selective approach to law enforcement**, with the police targeting some groups based on preconceived ideas rather than the actual likelihood of their offending.

This might explain the perception that Black drivers are disproportionately stopped by the police. This was reported by the British athlete **Bianca Williams** and the Labour MP **Dawn Butler** in 2020. Also in 2020, a video went viral of a driver in Ely, Cambridgeshire being stopped by police who told him: "*The reason I've stopped you is … – no offence to you, but you're a black male, OK, I'm not going to lie to you.*"

Research: find out more about **Stop & Search** and the cases mentioned above

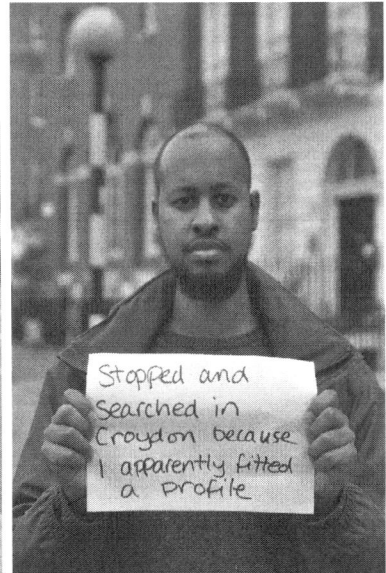

Stop & Search (photos: Darren Johnson/iDJ Photography)

RESEARCH PROFILE: SHAW (1930)

It's an old book, but **Clifford Shaw**'s *The Jack Roller* (1930) is an absolute classic in criminology. It's a self-report study of a Chicago delinquent named **Stanley**, between the ages 16-22. Stanley was interviewed by Shaw and contributed a 250-page description of his life; Shaw also obtained police and court papers to back up what Stanley told him.

Stanley starts stealing before he starts school, is a persistent truant and graduates in his teens to burglary and "Jack Rolling" (a slang term for robbing drunks and homosexual men who proposition him). He spends time in Detention Centres.

Stanley blames **external factors** for his offending: "*To start out in life, everyone has his chances— some good and some very bad … My start was handicapped by a no-good, ignorant, and selfish stepmother, who thought only of herself and her own children.*" Stanley's stepmother encourages him to steal but it is also a "*neighbourhood tradition*" in the deprived area where he grows up. Stanley runs away from home at age 6 to live on the streets, which he finds exciting and liberating.

Stanley also has an impulsive and thrill-seeking personality: "*How I loved to do these things! They thrilled me.*" However, he also picks up a criminal 'code' from the older boys and men he meets, which is **secondary socialisation by peers** into a **deviant subculture**. The strict discipline in reform schools only hardens him: "*I rebelled and harbored vengeance and hate.*"

At age 16, after leaving the Chicago House of Correction (prison), Stanley has a turning point. Shaw arranges for him to be fostered by a loving family; Stanley breaks off contact with his criminal friends, educates himself and finds a career; later he marries.

Jon Snodgrass (1972) tracked down Stanley before he died at age 75 and learned what became of him. Stanley lost his job in the Depression, divorced, returned to crime and spent time in a mental institution, but later remarried and retired. Stanley sums up his life saying: "*I would like to dwell on how fortunate I am to have lived through the early traumatic years and yet to have emerged relatively unscathed … I shall always remember, however, the humble days of adversity, living in the shadow of the horn of plenty.*"

Stanley's phrase 'living in the shadow of the horn of plenty' (a mythological symbol of wealth) links to **Philippe Bourgois (1995)** describing teenage crack-dealers in New York: "*the anguish of growing up poor in the richest city in the world*" and the idea of **relative deprivation** (p56).

Shaw's study is entirely **qualitative** data, using an **Interpretivist** methodology to explore the meaning of an offender's choices and circumstances. It is from a **Social Action** Perspective, with a focus on Stanley's freewill.

Research: find out more about the Jack Roller and Stanley's life; if you studied the **Youth Subculture**s option for **1B**, add this study to your notes on Interactionist explanations of youth deviance

EXAM PRACTICE: MEASURING CRIME & DEVIANCE

The OCR exam has three questions in **Paper 3 Section B**. Questions 7-9 are on Education and questions 10-12 are on Religion, Belief & Faith, but this Study Guide is focused on **Option 1** which covers questions **4-6**:

4. In what ways are crime and deviance relative? **[10 marks: 6 AO1 + 4 AO2]**

This is one of those 'describe & illustrate' questions, but with no Source A or Source B to lean on. No need to evaluate.

*Make **two** sociological points about relativism – perhaps from a Consensus and a Conflict viewpoint. It's a good idea to refer to named sociologists (like Durkheim, Marx, Weber, Pearson's **Hooligans** etc.) and you should definitely use some sociological terminology (like social solidarity, socialisation, ideology, superstructure). Then offer brief examples of relativism and make sure each example has an explanation of **why** it is relative. For example, "Stop & Search targets black drivers when the police view them as more likely not be criminals relative to white drivers."*

5. To what extent are official crime statistics trustworthy? **[20 marks: 8 AO1 + 4 AO2 + 8 AO3]**

This is a mid-size essay with a requirement for developed evaluation. You should spend 25 minutes and write at least 500 words.

*Write **three** points. Each point should introduce a sociological idea with some brief illustration from the real world. Each point should finish off with a developed evaluation (see **Chapter 5** for this). For example, you could write about OCS being standardised, the Dark Figure of unrecorded crime and the problem of police discretion. Make sure you mention **Holdaway**'s study on occupational culture in policing and be sure to answer the question: are OCS trustworthy or not?*

6. Outline and evaluate the problems in measuring crime effectively. **[40 marks: 16 AO1 + 8 AO2 + 16 AO3]**

This is the last of the two big (40 mark) essays in OCR A-Level Sociology. You should spend 50 minutes and write at least 1000 words.

*Write **five** points. Each point should introduce a sociological idea with some illustration from the real world. Each point should finish off with a developed evaluation (see **Chapter 5** for this). For example, you could write about the Dark Figure of unrecorded crime, then about OCS, victim surveys and self-report surveys and then finish with either the problem of police discretion or selective policing. Be sure to come to a conclusion: can we or can we not measure crime effectively?*

CHAPTER TWO – PATTERNS & TRENDS IN CRIME

The idea of patterns and trends in crime is clearly linked to **measuring crime** (pX). It's hard to write about one without bringing in the other. It's also linked to **theoretical explanations of crime** (p45) which offer reasons for these patterns and trends. It's a good idea to use these other ideas to evaluate patterns and trends in your essays. For example, if you write about a trend, you could evaluate it by explaining the problems of relying on **official crime statistics** (p16) or how this trend backs up or disproves a **Left Realist** explanation (p56). All patterns and trends can be criticised by bringing in the **Dark Figure** of unrecorded crime (p15).

*Some of the research from **Chapter 1** fits into this chapter too; for example, **Pearson**'s study of Hooligans shows trends over the centuries, **self-report studies** show patterns that are not in line with stereotypes and the **Islington Crime Survey** (p19) revealed surprising things about patterns of victimisation.*

The Great Crime Decline

After the Second World War, the UK and the USA were relatively law-abiding societies. However, from the 1950s to the 1970s crime rates increased steadily and reached an all-time high in the 1980s. There were fears that some American cities were becoming no-go areas and British inner cities had become dangerous places compared to previous decades.

In the USA, handgun-related homicides more than doubled between 1985-1990 and in 1990 there were a record 2245 murders in New York city alone.

Strangely, crime rates then started dropping. By 2000, the homicide rate in the USA had almost halved, violent crime dropped by a third and murders in New York went down by 75%.

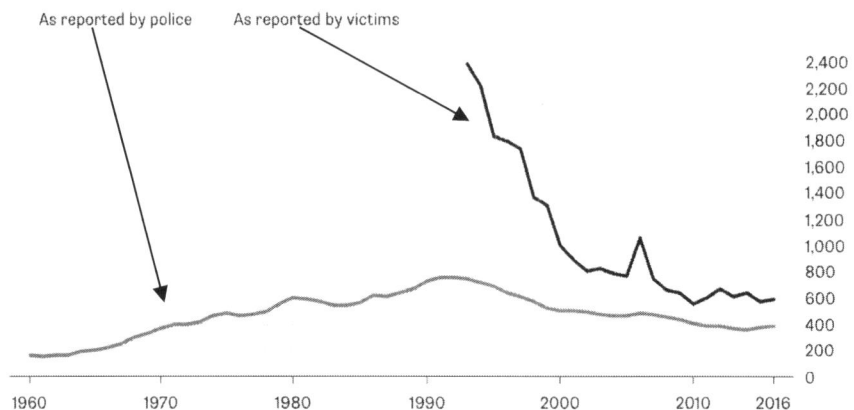

Sources: Federal Bureau of Investigation, Bureau of Justice Statistics
Does not include simple assaults where no weapon was used or no serious injury resulted.

Violent crime in the USA (per 100,000 population)

Something similar occurred in the UK, with crime rising throughout the 20th century and doubling in the 1960s, with an average of a million crimes reported each year, rising to 2 million in the 1970s and 3.5 million in the 1980s. Recorded offences reached 6 million in 2003 but have been dropping ever since (source: **Thompson et al., 2012**). The CSEW reports victimisation peaking earlier, in 1995, and dropping after that down to pre-1980s levels.

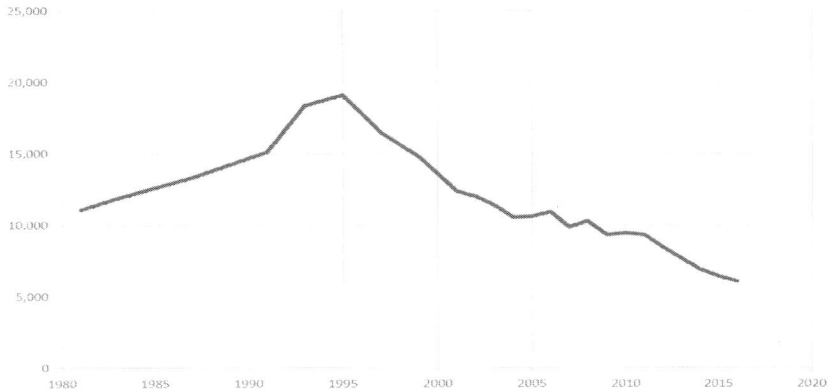

Crime in England and Wales from the CSEW (in 1000s of crimes)

The fall in crime is particularly surprising because it continued after the **Global Financial Crisis (GFC)** of **2008** which closed business and froze wages for many other people.

Criminologists are divided over the reasons for the Decline. Is it new technology like CCTV making crime more difficult (p66) or the Internet offering entertaining alternatives to crime? Is it tough **zero tolerance policing** (p68), **target hardening** (p65) or **welfare tackling poverty** (p75)? Or is it a reduction of lead in the air we breathe because of unleaded petrol in cars? Or (controversially) has the legalisation of abortion resulted in fewer unwanted children being born who would otherwise grow up to be criminals?

RESEARCH PROFILE: SHARKEY (2018)

Patrick Sharkey (2018) terms this drop in crime *"the Great Crime Decline"* and describes the period from the 1990s to today as an *"**Uneasy Peace**"* (the title of his book).

Sharkey links the Decline in the USA to tough policing and incarceration policies (currently the USA imprisons 0.7% of its population, which is a huge proportion, compared to 0.09% in the UK). He argues that although these policies have made deprived neighbourhoods safer, they also produce resentment and risk a backlash, which is why the peace is *"uneasy."*

Sharkey predicts the Decline will soon end. In 2020, in the middle of the 2020-21 Coronavirus Epidemic, the USA recorded the highest number of gun deaths in its history, which might be a sign of this happening.

*You could link this theory to **Shaw**'s study of Stanley (p22) who "harboured vengeance and hate" because of the strict discipline in reform schools – and also **Zero Tolerance Policing** (p68)*

PERSPECTIVES ON PATTERNS & TRENDS

Views on the meaning of patterns and trends vary from Perspective to Perspective but all have to grapple with the implications of the **Great Crime Decline** (p24).

CONSENSUS PERSPECTIVE: FUNCTIONALISM & NEW RIGHT

Functionalism places great faith in official statistics (it has a **positivist** view of research methods) and regards the patterns and trends revealed in statistics as **social facts** – direct insights into what is taking place in society. They do so even though the **Dark Figure** of unrecorded crime exists (p15) because they don't regard this unknown figure as changing the overall picture.

Functionalists take the **Great Crime Decline** at face value and link it to **progress** in society: better law enforcement, better standards of living, Capitalism ironing out its problems.

However, Functionalists have a complex relationship with crime. They regard crime as **inevitable** in society (p12) and as an indicator of **dysfunction**. If there is social dysfunction then crime will rise as an expression of it – and Functionalists believe there *is* dysfunction, such as high divorce rates and **strain** over available opportunities (p48). The **New Right** goes further than this, arguing that society is fundamentally broken by over-generous welfare and an **Underclass** producing delinquency and petty crime (p50).

Because of this, there *ought* to be increasing crime, not decreasing crime. The New Right focuses on trends linked to badly socialised youth, like **knife crime** (p38), and Functionalists focus on drug crimes and **'yobbish' behaviour**. They often claim that these crimes are 'swept under the carpet' by the police, with the reality on the streets being worse than it appears in statistics.

This puts the Consensus Perspective in the odd position of celebrating the decline of crime, while at the same time arguing that the important types of crime are increasing – and of claiming crime patterns and trends are social facts while insisting some of them are **socially constructed** (p12).

RESEARCH PROFILE: FALK ET AL. (2013)

Orjan Falk et al. (2013) carried out a study in Sweden and concluded that the majority of all violent crime is committed by a small number of people. They are almost all **male** (92%) with **substance abuse problems**, often **diagnosed with personality disorders**. The researchers examined 2.5 million people in Swedish criminal and population records between 1973-2004. They found that 4% were convicted of at least one violent crime, and 26% were re-convicted 3+ times; this leads to the conclusion that **1% of the population accounts for 63% of all violent crime convictions** during the period being studied.

This supports the Consensus view of a hard core of antisocial deviants driving up the worst crime figures. However, the results are only representative of Sweden in the 1973-2004 period and only account for convicted offenders; it ignores the Dark Figure of unrecorded crime and offenders who were not convicted (e.g. due to lack of evidence).

CONFLICT PERSPECTIVE: MARXISM & NEO-MARXISM

Marxism usually places great faith in statistics (especially to reveal **Inequality**) but abandons this positivist view when it comes to crime. Traditional Marxists regarded **official crime statistics** (p16) as a piece of fiction than crime reporting in the news to be propaganda. For them, the working classes are innocent, and the real criminals are the ruling classes.

Because Capitalism is **criminogenic** (creates crime because of its injustices) there ought to be lots of unreported crime: **white collar crime**, **corporate crime** (by businesses) and **state crime**.

Therefore, most Marxists are sceptical about the **Great Crime Decline** (p24) and the idea that Capitalism has 'fixed' itself.

Neo-Marxists have a rather more complicated view of patterns and trends in crime. **The Radical Criminology** school (p54) and **Left Realism** (p56) both accept that the statistics *do* reflect working-class crime. However, they contend that the media leads **moral panics** (p29) to exaggerate the extent of this sort of crime and also exaggerate Black crime. This is done to distract attention from economic problems in Capitalism and increase the fear of crime.

This means that **Neo-Marxists** are in the position of arguing that the **Great Crime Decline** is real and linking it to their successful policies (a Democrat President governed the USA in the 1990s and a Labour government came into power in the UK in 1997 through to 2010) while at the same time arguing that the statistics for crime are untrustworthy and exaggerated.

RESEARCH PROFILE: HALL (1978)

Stuart Hall is a **Neo-Marxist** who wrote *Policing The Crisis* **(1978)** at a time when the UK was rocked by strikes and suffering mass unemployment. Hall uses statistics to show that the fear of 'mugging' was unreasonable as the crime had gone *down* since the 1960s, not up, and was more likely to be carried out by White criminals. Hall points out that the British newspapers started a **moral panic** (p29) about **Black muggers** at a time when there was a genuine chance of Capitalism collapsing. This distracted people from the crisis, inflamed hostility between the White and Black working classes and justified police crackdowns.

This is termed the **'divide & rule'** approach to **social control** (p6): making marginalised groups (the White and Black working classes) hostile to each other so they never unite to challenge hegemonic power. The White working class welcome the deployment of heavy policing, because they believe (wrongly) it is protecting them.

Hall has been criticised for proposing a **conspiracy theory** without demonstrating exactly *how* the government and the newspaper editors organise to spread this false narrative. Nonetheless, the one-sidedness of news reporting is striking. Hall also assumes that the Black young men charged with mugging had been 'fitted up' by the police or provoked into resisting arrest but of course there might have been actual crimes and real victims.

CONFLICT PERSPECTIVE: FEMINISM

Feminists complain that patterns and trends in crime are misleading because they don't represent the full extent of the violence and harassment directed towards women. They do not think that this crime has meaningfully declined in the last 20 years so the **Great Crime Decline** (p24) has not reduced the victimisation of women.

4th Wave Feminism points to 'unofficial' victim survey, like the **2012 Sexual Assault Survey** by *Mumsnet* (pX) and more recently **Soma Sara's Everyone's Invited** website (**2020**), both of which invite women and girls to report their testimonies of sexual abuse.

Research: go back over your notes on **Peer Groups** as agencies of social control for **1A: Socialisation, Culture & Identity** and remind yourself about **Everyone's Invited**.

The problem is that the only evidence for these patterns and trends comes from victim surveys, many of which are highly **unstructured** and **unreliable**. There's no doubt that female victimisation is higher than **official crime statistics** show, but how much higher is not clear.

RESEARCH PROFILE: BATES (2014)

Laura Bates launched the Everyday Sexism Project online in 2012. The website invites women to contribute their personal stories of daily sexism, from street harassment to workplace discrimination to sexual assault and rape.

Bates expected to gather 100 testimonies, but the Project has collected over 100,000 testimonies and launched new branches in 25 countries worldwide.

Bates wrote a book also titled *Everyday Sexism* (2014) to reflect on the meaning of these testimonies of being groped on public transport or verbally abused by passing strangers.

Laura Bates (photo: Conway Hall)

Bates argues this behaviour is **normalised**: we accept it as normal, even though we shouldn't, which explains why it is **rarely reported**: "… *every woman I spoke to had a story. And they weren't random one-off events, but reams of tiny pinpricks – like my own experiences – so niggling and normalised that to protest about each one felt trivial. Yet put them together, and the picture was strikingly clear.*"

The idea of normalised sexually abusive behaviour is sometimes termed **'rape culture'** and it is an example of **social construction**: a criminal act that is not viewed as a crime.

Research: visit https://everydaysexism.com and reflect on some of the testimonies.

SOCIAL ACTION PERSPECTIVE: INTERACTIONISM

Interactionists view patterns and trends as part of the **social construction** of crime (p12). This means they tell us a lot about the attitudes and values of the people who define and measure crime, but not so much about what the public are doing.

For example, Labelling Theorists like **Howard Becker** regard 'criminal' as a social label that is applied to some people but not to others. If burglary has declined since 2003 (as trends suggest) then this doesn't necessarily mean that thieves have stopped breaking into people's houses; it just means victims no longer think it's worth involving the police (they contact their insurers instead) and the police no longer record such things as crimes.

On the other hand, if hate crimes have increased since 2016 (as trends suggest), it doesn't mean more bigots are attacking people that they discriminate against; it just means victims who used to regard themselves as having been assaulted or mugged as now considering themselves the victim of a hate crime and the police are increasingly recording it as such.

This means that the **Great Crime Decline** (p24) might really just be a decline in people reporting crimes and the police recording them.

This is an important insight into the social construction of crime and worth bearing in mind before you read too much into shocking figures about crime waves – but it tends to result in patterns and trends being dismissed as meaningless, which doesn't help with assessing crime prevention strategies or helping victims.

RESEARCH PROFILE: COHEN (1972)

Stan Cohen (1942–2013) wrote a classic in media studies, *Folk Devils & Moral Panics* **(1972)**. Cohen researched the fights which took place in English seaside resorts on Bank Holidays in 1964 between two youth subcultures: the **Mods** and the **Rockers**. Cohen's study was a mixture of observation, content analysis (looking at the language and images of the 1964 news reports) and interviews. He concludes that the media reporting was very different from the actual events, but it had a huge influence on the subsequent behaviour of the youths and the police. In effect, the Media *creates* the deviance rather than just reporting it.

Cohen suggests that there are five groups involved in the process of moral panic. There is the **threat** that starts the moral panic, which Cohen calls a "**folk devil.**" There are **enforcers of laws**, like the police. There is the **news media** reporting on it and attaching symbolic images to it. There are **politicians**, who sometimes add to the panic. Finally, there is **the public**, which becomes concerned about the threat and demands something be done about it.

This study supports the idea that news stories are **socially constructed** rather than **social facts** and that the reporting of crime influences the way statistics are compiled. However, it might not be representative of interactive and video-driven 21st century news.

PATTERNS & TRENDS: A TOOLKIT

You are expected to know about four main types of patterns/trends and could be asked to focus on either **offending** (who is committing crimes) or **victimisation** (who the victims are). Most research suggests that the average offender and the average victim are very similar: male, working class and aged 18-24. They are disproportionately likely to be Black.

SOCIAL DISTRIBUTION BY SOCIAL CLASS

We have already seen that **self-report studies** show that offending behaviour in working class and middle classes youths is very similar (p21). However, there is a perception that crime is a working class phenomenon, with the middle classes viewed as 'respectable' and 'law abiding.' Fear of crime is high among middle class households, who own expensive possessions and invest in security measures like burglar alarms. But do the figures bear this stereotype out?

Offending

According to **National Prison Survey (2020)**, 41% of male convicts come from unskilled or skilled manual classes. **Robert Reiner (2007)** claims that 74% of the prison population is drawn from the poorest 20% of the population.

According to the **Mayor of London's Office (2019)**, three-quarters of the boroughs in London with the highest levels of violent offending are also in the top 10 most deprived, while the same boroughs also have higher proportions of children living in poverty than the London average. This certainly links crime to deprivation and low social class.

The main criticism is that these patterns reflect who gets caught rather than who offends. Wealthy and educated offenders are more likely to carry out crimes that go undetected (e.g. **white collar crime**) and avoid conviction if caught because they can afford good lawyers.

Victimisation

The **CSEW** (p19) doesn't collect data on social class of victims but there are other measures. For example, in 2020, only 1.2% of homeowners were victims of violent crime but this rose to 2.5% for people privately renting, doubling the risk. Home ownership is associated with the wealthy middle class and poorer people are more likely to rent.

The two groups most at risk of violent crime are the unemployed and students (source: **ONS, 2020**). Since students are more likely to be middle class than working class, this suggests that a similar lifestyle is the main factor, such as being out late, traveling on foot/public transport rather than driving, living in poorer neighbourhoods and living in insecure accommodation.

Research: visit https://www.ons.gov.uk/visualisations/dvc432/content.html and input different background details into the **Risk of Crime Calculator**

AO2 ILLUSTRATION: THE SHANNON MATTHEWS CASE

In 2008, 10-year-old **Shannon Matthews** disappeared from her home in West Yorkshire, followed by appeals on national TV from her mother Karen. 24 days later Shannon was discovered by the police in a house belonging to a relative of Karen Matthew's boyfriend. It soon became clear that Karen Matthews had arranged her daughter's disappearance (and kept her sedated with a travel sickness drug) in order for the relative to claim the £50,000 reward for later finding her.

There was a lot of public outrage and much of it was directed at the chaotic family life that Shannon grew up in. The Matthews family, living on benefits and trying to make money out of their children, resembled the **Underclass** described by the **New Right** (p50) as well as the stereotype of immoral **Chavs** that was popular at the time.

Some commentators pointed out how the local working class community had united to search for missing Shannon, but this had received very little praise in the news media. The story illustrates working class families as both offenders *and* victims, but also the way in which the media stigmatises the working classes (i.e. presents them negatively).

RESEARCH PROFILE: JONES (2011)

Owen Jones is a Marxist journalist and activist whose book *Chavs* (2011) exposes negative stereotyping of the poor. 'Chavs' was a term popular in the early 2000s for anti-social youths from deprived backgrounds, wearing sportswear and (often counterfeit) brands like Burberry. Chav seems to come from a Romany word for 'youth' but it is (wrongly) interpreted as being a code for Council Housed And Violent.

Jones argues that middle class contempt for 'Chavs' is another example of **stigmatising** the working classes and a **moral panic** fuelled by the news media. The effect is to divide the working class against each other and justify excluding them from politics, public places and serious consideration.

Jones' argument resembles **Pearson**'s study of Hooligans (p14), **Cohen**'s earlier study of Mods and Rockers as folk devils in the 1960s (p29) and **Hall**'s study of the Black mugger as a scapegoat in the 1970s (p27). Jones has been criticised for treating the working class as homogeneous and not recognising their freewill. **Lynsey Hanley (2011)** points out that that *"a great deal of chav-bashing goes on within working-class neighbourhoods."*

SOCIAL DISTRIBUTION BY GENDER

The gender divide in crime is stark, with males overwhelmingly being the main offenders and also most likely to be victims. This is often linked to characteristics like aggression and risk-taking in males, due either to **biological factors** (like the male hormone testosterone) or **socialisation** (with females socialised to be more compliant). However, this divide can be questioned.

Offending

Official crime statistics consistently show males responsible for at least 80% of crimes. In 2019, males make up 85% of all arrests and women are more likely to appear in court for less severe offences, like driving offences which make up 55% of females but only 29% of males. The average male prison sentence is 19.7 months compared to 11.3 months for females. Males are responsible for 74% of violent crime (source: **ONS, 2019**).

The Youth Justice Board (2009) shows that the peak age for female offending is 15, but it is 18 for males. This suggests that females start deviant behaviour earlier (but perhaps with less serious transgressions) then grow out of it, whereas male deviance continues into their 20s with much more serious consequences.

However, female offending (so-called 'pink collar crime') seems to be rising. According to the **Institute for Criminal Policy Research (2017)**, in the 21st century the global female prison population increased by a half while males went up by a fifth.

This shift might be due to increasing gender equality in society and women experiencing many of the same economic pressures as men (e.g. being the breadwinner for the household) or technology like the Internet making crime more accessible to women.

The **Chivalry Thesis** (p32) offers another view: women are treated more leniently by police and the courts due to gender stereotyping and **police discretion**, so their offending does not get recorded to the same degree as men. To combat this, **Europol (2019)** invited 21 EU states to submit their 'most wanted' fugitive for a '*Crime Has No Gender*' campaign and 18 were female.

Research: visit Europol's '*Crime Has No Gender*' campaign at https://www.europol.europa.eu/newsroom/news/crime-has-no-gender-meet-europe%E2%80%99s-most-wanted-female-fugitives and study the 'most wanted' offenders

Victimisation

Males make up 3.9% of victims of crime, compared to females 3.4%. 64% of homicide victims are male, compared to 36% being female. Men are twice as likely to be victims of violent crime (experienced by 2.3% compared to 1.2% of women). However, when it comes to crimes like domestic abuse, victimisation rises to 7.3% for females and 3.6% for males, doubling the female risk (source: **ONS, 2019**).

Moreover, the **Islington Crime Survey** (p19) revealed in stark terms the 'curfew on women' imposed by the fear of crime and sexual assault after dark. The campaigning organisation **Femicide (2018)** carried out a census showing 1428 women were killed by men over 10 years, which is one killing every three days. 4.9 million women report sexual assault in their lives and 1.4 million have faced rape; the figures for men are a fifth of that, while 98.5% of rapists are male (source: **ONS, 2021**).

AO2 ILLUSTRATION: THE MURDER OF SARAH EVERARD

In 2021, 33-year-old **Sarah Everard** was abducted and murdered when walking home at night past Clapham Common in London. The murderer turned out to be a serving Metropolitan police officer. The case prompted outrage regarding the violence directed at women by men and the dangers for women in traveling freely. A vigil held for Sarah Everard was attended by many Feminist groups but there was controversy when it was forcefully dispersed by the police (due to restrictions on assembling during the 2020-21 Coronavirus Pandemic).

A later protest was called the **97 March** after a survey for **UN Women (2021)** revealed that 97% of women have been sexually harassed. **Baroness Jenny Jones** made the suggestion that there should be a **'curfew on men'** which would *"make women a lot safer."* Jones' argument was that instead of expecting women to restrict themselves to be safe (not leaving home after dark, not traveling alone), we should expect men to experience these inconveniences since they are the perpetrators. The fact that women are blamed if they fail to protect themselves reveals the **social construction** of crime (p12).

RESEARCH PROFILE: ADLER (1975)

Freda Adler is a Feminist who wrote *Sisters In Crime* (1975). She examines data from the 1960s to show a growing trend for female criminality and she predicts that this trend will accelerate. Adler proposes a **Liberation Thesis** that growing freedom for women enables them to leave the domestic sphere (the home) and find work. This causes them to develop traditionally masculine traits like aggression and risk-taking and exposes them to opportunities for committing crime that never used to be available.

Adler's argument resembles a **Functionalist** one – that crime is regrettable, but it is a necessary side-effect of something good, which is progress. She is supported by **Carolyn Jackson (2006)** who reports a growing culture of 'Laddish' behaviour in schoolgirls.

However, Adler's original data set was too small to draw confident conclusions from and female crime has not accelerated as she predicted. **Estrada et al. (2015)** suggests that women are not becoming more like men but rather the other way around: the offending rate for men is dropping, closing the gender gap with women.

SOCIAL DISTRIBUTION BY ETHNICITY

In the **2011 Census**, 83% of the UK population identify as White, 8% Asian and 3% Black. You would expect this distribution to appear in crime figures too, with 83% of offences carried out by White people and 83% of the victims of crime being White. The fact that this distribution does *not* appear is troubling for sociologists.

Offending

The arrest rate for the White population is 10 arrests per 1,000 people; this rises to 18 for Mixed Race and 32 for Black. This is a startling difference in arrests. The rate for the Asian population in the UK is 12 (only 6 for Indian) and the lowest rate is 3 per 1,000 people for Chinese. 21% of those convicted of homicide are Black compared to 67% White (source: **ONS, 2019**).

Similarly, 73% of the UK prison population identity as White and 27% as Black, Asian or other minority ethnic groups (source: **Ministry of Justice, 2019**).

One explanation for this is that these populations commit more crime. This is the explanation preferred by **Functionalists** who treat such data as **social facts**. In support of this, ethnicity tends to intersect with **social class**, with Black populations in the UK being more likely to be poor and Indian and Chinese more likely to be wealthy.

However, another explanation is **institutional (or systemic) racism** in the criminal justice system (CJD). The police might be more likely to stop and search Black youths, more like to arrest them if they see something suspicious and courts might be more likely to convict them of offences. **Geoff Pearson & Mike Rowe (2020)** spent 7 years observing UK police officers carrying out stop & search and conclude its use with Black suspects is disproportionate. **Holdaway**'s research (p17) found a racist occupational culture in the Metropolitan police in the 1970s.

Hall's study of racist moral panics in the news (p27) points out that there are pressures from the news media to target Black suspects.

However, the argument for racist bias in the CJD struggles to account for the low rate of offending in Indian or Chinese ethnic groups.

Victimisation

Most ethnic groups have broadly similar levels of victimisation (13% on average) but the Mixed Ethnicity group stands out for the high rate of victimisation: 21% for males and 19% for females (source: **ONS, 2020**).

However, Black people in the UK have a higher risk of being victims of homicide, 5.6 times higher than White people throughout the 21st century and increasing since 2015. This experience **intersects with age**, with Black youths aged 16-24 being 10.6 times more likely to be victims of homicide: 49% of Black victims, compared to 25% Asian or 12% White (source: **ONS, 2019**).

There is a tendency for crime to be **intra-racial**. This means offenders are more likely to commit crimes against people of the **same** racial group as themselves. This might explain the high victimisation for Mixed Race individuals, if they belong to more than one group.

AO2 ILLUSTRATION: THE MURDER OF STEPHEN LAWRENCE

Stephen Lawrence was 18 years old when he was killed in 1993 in a racist attack. He had been waiting for a bus with a friend, when a gang of White racists attacked them both. Stephen's friend escaped and called the police, but Stephen died from his injuries.

The Metropolitan Police's investigation was flawed from the start. For example, their initial suspect was Stephen's friend. They did not pursue the gang, although they were already known racists. When the suspects were brought to trial, the case collapsed because of weak evidence collected by the police.

Eventually, in 2012, two of Stephen's killers were convicted when new evidence emerged. Before that, in 1999, the **Macpherson Report** (p57) into the case concluded that the Metropolitan Police were "*institutionally racist*" (echoing accusation made by **Holdaway** in the 1970s, p17). Dr Neville Lawrence said that his son's murder "*opened the country's eyes*" to racism.

The case of Stephen Lawrence suggests that the way crimes against Black people are investigated makes it hard to know whether the **social distribution of crime by ethnicity** is reliably measured.

Research: find out more about Stephen Lawrence, the police investigation and its outcomes

RESEARCH PROFILE: FITZGERALD ET AL. (2002)

Marion Fitzgerald and colleagues conducted the **Policing for London Survey** in the aftermath of the **Stephen Lawrence** case. They interviewed people stopped by the Metropolitan Police and found many were satisfied with their treatment but measured a decline in confidence in the police during the 1980s and 1990s. Dissatisfaction with the police was highest among three groups: young people, Black people and people living in deprived areas. The best predictors of being stopped by the police were "*being young, being male, being black, being working class and being single*" – which indicates how patterns in crime are affected by **Intersectionality**.

This supports the contention that policing practices are **institutionally racist**. It only describes the Metropolitan Police of 20 years ago and doesn't account for reforms since then, such as the Metropolitan Police recruiting Black and minority ethnic officers.

SOCIAL DISTRIBUTION BY AGE

In 1901, the UK population had a high proportion of children (32% aged under 15) and a small elderly population (only 5% aged 65+). In 2018, the proportions of people in these two age groups were the same (18% for each). This shows the UK has an ageing population: people are living longer and having fewer children (source: **ONS, 2020**).

As society has more and more elderly people in it and proportionally fewer young people, you would expect this to affect patterns and trends of crime, with less crime by the young but more elderly victims of crime. However, these patterns aren't obvious.

Offending

Stereotypes have always presented adolescents and young adults as impulsive and rule-breaking, compared to more retrained and law-abiding older people. Crime increases in early adolescence (age 14), peaks in the 20s, and then declines. This statistical shape has been termed the **age–crime curve (Roque et al, 2015)**.

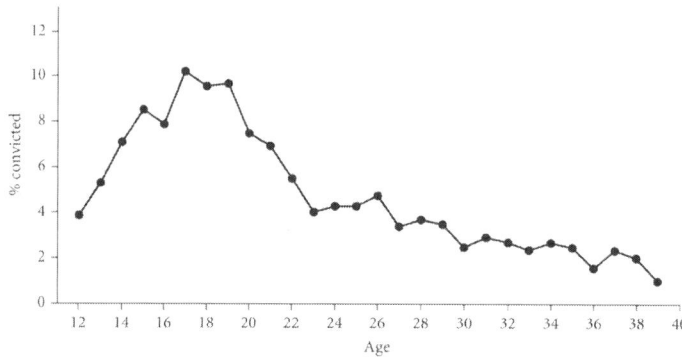

*An example of the age-crime curve from the famous Cambridge Study (**Farrington et al, 1995**)*

Declining proportions of young people in society might explain the **Great Crime Decline** (p24). However, prison populations tell a different story, with 30-39 year olds making up 32% of UK prisoners, with much smaller numbers of younger and older convicts.

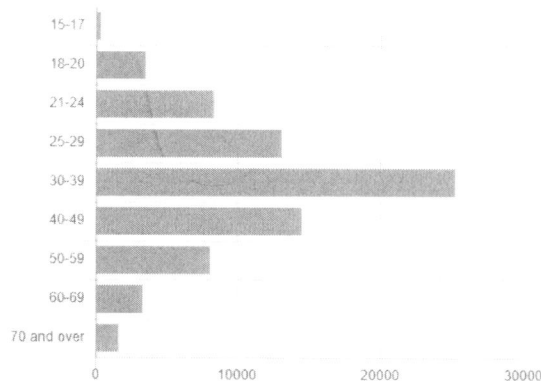

Prison population by age band (source: Ministry of Justice, 2021)

This is probably because more serious crimes (and a history of previous offending) make it more likely a person will get a custodial (prison) sentence; also, prisoners on long sentences might have entered prison when they were much younger. According to the **Joseph Rowntree Foundation (JRF)** only about 5% of males are **chronic offenders** who persist in criminal behaviour, going on to become long-term prisoners, but the majority of young people abandon crime as they get older.

Victimisation

Young people are certainly at risk of victimisation: those aged 20-29 made up 13% of the UK population but are the victims in 27% of violent crimes; people aged 80+ make up 5% of the population but are victims in less than 1% of violent crimes (source: **ONS, 2021**). As with **social class** (p30), this is certainly linked to lifestyle, with older people more likely to stay at home in secure accommodation and avoid traveling on foot, at night or interacting often with strangers.

Young women aged 20-24 are more likely to be victims of domestic abuse (15.1% of cases) than older women – and women aged 16-19 are the next most victimised group for this (source: **ONS, 2019**).

Older people are more likely to be victims of crimes like fraud, with 12% of people aged 65+ reporting being victims of fraud in a year; the elderly make up 8 out of every 10 victims of doorstep scams (source: **ONS, 2019**).

There is little evidence to support the idea that older people have more **fear of crime**, but they do perceive themselves to be more **vulnerable** to crime and take more precautions against it, which perhaps explains why they are less likely to be victims (source: **Köber et al, 2020**).

Zombie knives (photo: Flossy Carter)

AO2 ILLUSTRATION: KNIFE CRIME

In 2020, there were 46,000 knife crimes, 51% higher than in 2011 when the government started keeping track of knife crimes specifically – and that figure excludes Greater Manchester Police which could not provide data. According to the CSEW, knives account for 9% of all violent crime and 1 in 5 such attackers are under 18. The majority of the attacks are in London (source: **ONS, 2020**).

Various factors are blamed for the 'epidemic' of knife crime in UK cities: disputes between drug-dealing gangs, social media glorifying violence, the closure of youth clubs and mental health issues brought on by lockdowns during the 2020-21 Coronavirus Pandemic. Others blame the declining use of Stop & Search by the police. In 2016, the sale of **'Zombie Knives'** was banned: these giant blades with serrated edges are collected by horror fans but were used in attacks.

Research: find out more about the increase in knife crimes and plans to deal with it

RESEARCH PROFILE: FARRINGTON ET AL. (2006)

David Farrington conducted the famous **Cambridge Study** which is a massive longitudinal study of 411 boys from the East End of London who were born in 1953-4. The study began when the boys were 8-9. It involved interviews with the boys, their parents and teachers as well as gathering medical data, school reports and police reports.

There were follow-up **self-report** interviews as the cohort aged. By age 48, 93% were still alive and interviewed. Of this group of 404, 360 had criminal records. Their offending had peaked at age 17. A small number (7%) were defined as **chronic offenders** because they accounted for half of the offences recorded by the study: on average, their criminal careers lasted from age 14-35.

The proportion leading successful (non-criminal) lives was 78% at age 32 but rose to 88% at 48 – the reformed offenders were no different in life success from the ones with no convictions.

There are lots of dates for the Cambridge Study, which is updated regularly, but big reports came out in 1982, 1995 and this data is from 2006.

Farrington concludes that the factors involved in criminality are family histories of crime, poverty, impulsive personality traits, poor parenting and poor school performance. He recommends targeting at-risk children to reduce future offending.

Farrington's study only considers males from a White working class background. Despite this, Farrington's results closely resemble national patterns today in the life course of offenders. Another longitudinal self-report study, the **Edinburgh Study of Youth Transitions and Crime (ESYTC)**, has a cohort of 4300 young people who started secondary school in 1998. This study focuses on gender difference and has a cohort from 'this side' of the **Great Crime Decline** (p24), but they are still too old to have grown up through the knife crime epidemic.

GLOBAL PATTERNS: ORGANISED CRIME

Globalisation is explored in **3A: Globalisation & the Digital Social World**. It challenges ideas about crime because crime is normally defined as breaking a country's laws, but global crime goes beyond any one country. There are some international crime agencies that seek out and punish such criminals (e.g. **Interpol**) but global crime is also tackled by military intervention; e.g. after the 911 bombings, the USA and allies invaded Afghanistan, where the terrorist organisers were based.

As well as terrorism, global organised crime is involved in drug smuggling, people trafficking, arms dealing, cyber crime and identity theft, kidnapping, counterfeiting and extortion (threatening people to get money). It includes people smugglers sending migrants across the sea in dinghies, scammers emailing you from Nigeria and pirates capturing ships off the coast of Somalia. It also includes famous crime cartels like the **Mafia**. The **Global Financial Integrity Report (2017)** states that *"transnational crime is a business, and business is very good"* and estimates that global crime makes between $1.6-2.2 *trillion* a year.

A trillion is a thousand billion. If you stacked a trillion dollars, the pile would stretch all the way to the sun. With a trillion dollars, you could buy the oil company Exxon Mobil and have enough left to buy McDonald's and Coca-Cola too.

Hobbs & Dunningham (1998) studied how organised crime has expanded from large but national crime organisations to transnational crime organisations on the back of globalisation. They suggest that this has led to the decline of tightly organised groups like the Mafia. Instead, global crime operates through a **'glocal'** system –a global network built from local connections. For example, local opium-growers deliver their product to a drug cartel with an international supply chain (with enough wealth and power to get the product over national borders) which then sells heroin on to local dealers at the other end.

AO2 ILLUSTRATION: THE MAFIA

The term 'Mafia' is used for any organised crime group, but the word comes from Sicily and was used to describe the *Cosa Nostra*, a Sicilian crime subculture. The **American Mafia** became powerful and wealthy smuggling alcohol during 1920s Prohibition; it was linked to Italian-American families and included the famous gangster **Al Capone**. These Mafia groups were often based around family ties, with a boss (*don*), his lieutenants (*capos*) and their soldiers. The groups maintained a code of *omerta* (secrecy). However, in the 1980s and '90s a number of high profile cases in Italy and the USA convicted powerful Mafia leaders by getting gangsters to break the *omerta* code and testify against each other.

Since then, new Mafia organisations have appeared, notably in the former-USSR, such as the **Russian Mafia** and **Bulgarian Mafia**. However, these groups operate more like businesses than families and don't have the rituals, honour-code or link to a supportive community base.

RESEARCH PROFILE: GLENNY (2008)

Misha Glenny wrote the book *McMafia* **(2008)**, examining the way organised crime adapts to Globalisation. The title links to **Ritzer**'s concept of '**McDonaldisation**' in society (*c.f.* **3A: Globalisation & the Digital Social World**) and suggests that organised crime has transformed in the same way. The book inspired a 2018 TV drama series.

Glenny suggests that organised criminal gangs have become very influential in areas of the world where there is **weak rule of law** (e.g. failed states such as Afghanistan), widespread **distrust of the state** (e.g. Mexico), a landscape that makes areas **inaccessible** (e.g. Colombia with its rainforest) and high levels of **corruption**.

Glenny argues that a significant criminal network operates from **Bulgaria**, which is a 'hub' connecting the rich and poor parts of the world. The Mafia have held considerable power there since the collapse of Communism in 1989. Glenny links the Bulgarian Mafia to most of the drugs and prostitutes that are bought in the UK.

Glenny explores other networks, such as gunrunners in Ukraine, money launderers in Dubai, drug syndicates in Canada and cyber criminals in Brazil. Glenny takes a **Marxist** approach that this crime is generated by Capitalism itself. He argues that, since drugs account for 70% of the profits of global crime, legalising drugs would be the best way of reducing the power of these criminals. However, he underestimates the importance of **glocalisation** because he makes organisations like the Mafia so important to his analysis.

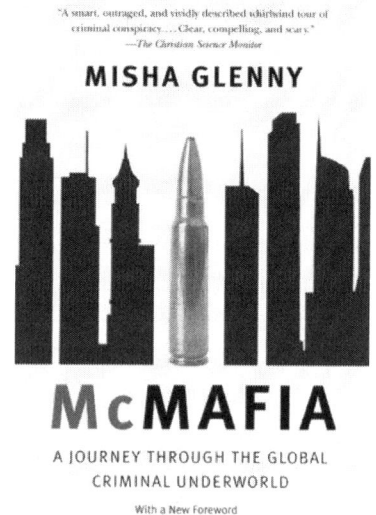

"A smart, outraged, and vividly described whirlwind tour of criminal conspiracy.... Clear, compelling, and scary."
—*The Christian Science Monitor*

MISHA GLENNY

McMAFIA

A JOURNEY THROUGH THE GLOBAL
CRIMINAL UNDERWORLD

With a New Foreword

GLOBAL PATTERNS: GREEN CRIME

Green crime – or environmental crime – is also linked to **Globalisation** as environmental damage caused in one country can affect its neighbours or even the entire planet. It includes illegal pollution and dumping toxic waste but also **poaching** and the destruction of endangered species. Poaching is part of a multimillion-dollar industry that is part of **organised global crime**. However, a lot of environmental damage is caused by legitimate businesses 'cutting corners' and ignoring regulations that are supposed to protect the environment for the sake of profit.

'Green crime' is a term coined by **Michael J Lynch (1990)** and it is an example of **transgressive criminology**. This means that many of the 'crimes' studied here are not literally crimes – or else they occupy loop-holes or grey areas in international law – but transgressive criminologists argue that since they cause harm on a global scale, they are transgressions (wrong-doing) that should be treated as crimes. These criminologists are also activists, trying to change laws to make such things literally illegal instead of just transgressive.

Rob White (2008) divides green crime into two types of harm.

- **Anthropocentric Harm:** harm to the environment from the perspective of humanity; e.g. pollution damages the water supply or causes diseases that then harms humans.
- **Ecocentric Harm:** sees harm to any aspect of the environment as transgressive whether it impacts humans or not; e.g. animal cruelty or the destruction of habitats, regardless of whether there is any specific human cost.

Nigel South (2008) talks about two other types of green crime:

- **Primary Green Crime:** is committed directly against the environment or causes harm to the environment; e.g. pollution, deforestation, animal cruelty
- **Secondary Green Crime:** undermines the rules regarding protecting the environment, e.g: violence against environmental groups, bribery/corruption to get round regulations

Transgressive criminology is difficult to put into practice. By focusing on 'harm' rather than laws, the idea of Green Crime becomes very **subjective**; almost anything can be Green Crime. For example, should *all* meat production or even consumption of meat be a Green Crime, or just meat farmed with cruel methods?

Nonetheless, the idea of transgressive criminology is popular with **Conflict** sociologists who regard the actual laws as the creations of privileged groups (**Marxists** point to wealthy Capitalists, **Feminists** point to men) and see the job of a sociologists to question the **social construction** (p12) of law. **Consensus** sociologists see laws as the expression of our culture and are inclined to view Green Crime as a crime if it breaks laws, but not as any sort of crime at all if it doesn't.

Rainbow Warrior (photo: Hans van Dijk)

AO2 ILLUSTRATION: GREENPEACE & *RAINBOW WARRIOR*

Greenpeace is a non-governmental campaigning group founded in 1971 and based out of the Netherlands but with offices in 55 countries. It campaigns for the protection of the environment and the exposing and prevention of Green Crime. Its aim is to *"ensure the ability of the Earth to nurture life in all its diversity."* It opposes climate change, deforestation, overfishing, whaling, genetic engineering and nuclear power.

You will notice that not all of Greenpeace's targets fit the ordinary definition of a crime and some (like nuclear power) are presented by other groups as solutions to environmental problems – this shows transgressive criminology in action but also the problem with it.

Greenpeace uses boats to protest over-fishing, commercial whaling and nuclear testing at sea and *Rainbow Warrior* was the flagship. In 1985, *Rainbow Warrior* sailed to New Zealand to protest French nuclear testing in the Pacific. The French Intelligence Service (DGSE) planted bombs on the ship and sank it. A photographer on board was killed, two French spies were arrested, and France paid Greenpeace $8.1 million in compensation.

The sinking of *Rainbow Warrior* is an example of a **secondary green crime**.

RESEARCH PROFILE: BECK (1992)

Ulrich Beck published *The Risk Society* **(1992)** in response to the 1988 nuclear disaster at **Chernobyl**, in which a nuclear reactor leaked radioactive pollution across Europe. Beck explains Green Crime as part **'the risk society,'** arguing that industrial societies create new risks because of modern technologies that were unknown in the past. Because we have no previous experiences of risks of this sort, we are not well equipped to weigh them up or manage them.

*Do Beck's ideas sound familiar? They are echoed by **Giddens'** concept of **manufactured risk** that was introduced in **3A: Globalisation & the Digital Social World**.*

Beck claims that one new 'risky technology' is nuclear power, which generates small quantities of highly toxic waste which stays radioactive for thousands of years. Beck argues that environmental problems are global – he states that *"smog is democratic"* meaning that pollution affects everyone equally regardless of your background.

Beck doesn't offer any solutions to the problem of Green Crime; he just points out that this is a new problem that cannot be tackled using traditional ideas and policies. This means he supports **transgressive criminology** rather than the view that environmental crime is just another type of global crime – or not really a crime at all.

*Beck isn't strictly a **Postmodernist** – like Giddens, he believes we are in **Late Modernity** – but his ideas about risk resemble a Postmodern diagnosis of contemporary problems.*

AO2 ILLUSTRATION: THE 2011 LONDON RIOTS

In the summer of 2011, there was a week of rioting in towns and cities across England, but largely in London and starting in Tottenham. TV viewers were shocked to see battles with the police, the burning of cars, buses and shops as well as looting on a huge scale. There were 5 deaths and over £200 million in property damage.

The police made over 3000 arrests and courts had to open for extended hours to process all the cases. An instruction came from the Conservative Government that rioters be punished with strong sentences, including 4 years for a man who stayed home but encouraged rioting via *Facebook*.

While 12% of the working-age population of the UK are on benefits of some sort, 35% of the adults prosecuted after the riots were on benefits. Some commentators took this as evidence for the link between class and crime – or for the **New Right**'s idea of the crime-prone **Underclass** (pX).

While 49% of the population of the UK in 2011 were male, 90% of the adults prosecuted after the riots were male. This could be evidence for the link between males and crime.

While 3% of the population of the UK in 2011 was Black – rising to 11% in London as a whole – 50% of the adults prosecuted after the riots were Black. Some commentators took this as evidence for the link between ethnicity and crime – or for the **Neo-Marxist** idea of the police targeting Black working class people disproportionately through **selective policing** (p21).

London riots (photo: StuartBannock)

EXAM PRACTICE: PATTERNS & TRENDS IN CRIME

The OCR exam has three questions in **Paper 3 Section B**. Questions 7-9 are on Education and questions 10-12 are on Religion, Belief & Faith, but this Study Guide is focused on **Option 1** which covers questions **4-6**:

4. In what ways is victimisation distributed by gender? **[10 marks: 6 AO1 + 4 AO2]**

This is one of those 'describe & illustrate' questions, but with no Source A or Source B to lean on. No need to evaluate.

Make two sociological points about victimisation – perhaps a point about males and a point about females. It's a good idea to refer to particular statistics (like 64% of homicide victims being male) and you should definitely use some sociological terminology (like the Dark Figure or the Great Crime Decline). Then offer examples of victimisation and make sure each example has an explanation linked to gender. For example, "Males are more at risk from homicide and this might be because they are also more likely to commit homicide."

5. To what extent is green crime a growing problem? **[20 marks: 8 AO1 + 4 AO2 + 8 AO3]**

This is a mid-size essay with a requirement for developed evaluation. You should spend 25 minutes and write at least 500 words.

*Write **three** points. Each point should introduce a sociological idea with some illustration from the real world. Each point should finish off with a developed evaluation (see **Chapter 5** for this). For example, you could write about ecocentric crimes, secondary green crimes and transgressive criminology. Make sure you mention **Beck**'s study on risk and be sure to answer the question: are green crimes growing or not?*

6. Outline and evaluate the view that ethnicity is important for understanding patterns and trends in crime. **[40 marks: 16 AO1 + 8 AO2 + 16 AO3]**

This is the last of the two big (40 mark) essays in OCR A-Level Sociology. You should spend 50 minutes and write at least 1000 words.

*Write **five** points. Each point should introduce a sociological idea with some illustration from the real world. Each point should finish off with a developed evaluation (see Chapter 5 for this). For example, you could write about the ethnic groups as offenders, then as victims, then the Dark Figure of unrecorded crime, police institutional racism and finish with either **Fitzgerald et al.** or **Holdaway** criticising the Metropolitan Police. Be sure to come to a conclusion: is ethnicity important or is class, age or gender more significant?*

CHAPTER THREE – EXPLAINING CRIME & DEVIANCE

Cr8ime and deviance can be explained by a number of *"theoretical views"* that match the Perspectives you have learned about earlier in the course. However, a few new criminology Perspectives are introduced as well: **Realism (Left & Right)** and **Subcultural Theories**.

Positive Views of Crime & Deviance

It might seem strange to have a 'positive' view of crime, especially if you've been a victim of it. However, crime has its up-sides and not just for the criminals.

Crime stimulates the economy because stolen or vandalised goods have to be replaced, often with superior one. This means a demand for manufacturing, trade in the shops and income for insurance companies. People also buy security equipment (locks, alarms, CCTV).

Crime reinforces communities, which band together in adversity. Neighbourhood Watch schemes encourage people to keep an eye on each other's property and entire communities come together during crises (like the townsfolk searching for the missing **Shannon Matthews**, p31). When people discuss crime and express their outrage and pity, they reinforce society's norms and values.

Crime can act as a way for people to 'vent' frustrations and express unhappiness. This argument is often used with respect to prostitution, asserting (often without evidence) that if men did not visit prostitutes, they would commit rape. A less controversial example is rioting, which expresses dissatisfaction with the police and/or the government and can be a trigger for social reform.

This viewpoint is associated with **Functionalism** (p47) but **Neo-Marxists** argue that crime is important resistance to Capitalism (p54) and **4th Wave Feminists** sometimes argue that sex work is empowering for women (p58 and see the ideas of **Adler**, p33).

Negative Views of Crime & Deviance

A more common view is that crime is a bad thing, a cause of misery and fear, and it needs to be prevented wherever possible.

An important point made by **Left Realists** (p56) is that the rich have the wherewithal to replace stolen property and make themselves secure. Poor people, on the other hand, carry on suffering from the effects of crime even after the crime is over: lost goods, damaged self-esteem, insecurity, lost income while recovering. This is termed **multiple victimisation**, since the poor are hurt by crime in many more ways than the rich.

A similar point is made by **Feminists**, that crime is part of a culture of violent intimidation that oppresses women, restricts their movement and makes them dependent on men for protection (an uncertain protection, since male partners are the main source of domestic and sexual violence for women).

Even **Functionalists** have limits to the amount of crime they will tolerate as 'healthy' and they acknowledge that when crime becomes excessive, society becomes **dysfunctional**. The idea that society has already reached (or surpassed) this point of dysfunction is key to understanding the **New Right** Perspective (p50).

AO2 ILLUSTRATION: THE AMERICAN OPIOID EPIDEMIC

A crime problem that illustrates these views is the addiction to opioids in America. **Opioids** are pain-killing drugs that were heavily prescribed in the 1990s; they are strong, cheap but very addictive and an overdose can kill. Because they produce feelings of euphoria, they are popular as recreational drugs. They are supposed to be prescribed only to manage acute (temporary) pain, but America's private healthcare system combined with a black market means people can easily get long-term prescriptions or buy opioids illegally, often moving on to more dangerous opioids like heroin and fentanyl.

In 2020, nearly 70,000 Americans died from overdoses (more than die from motor accidents or shootings). Celebrities like the musicians Prince and Tom Petty and the actor Heath Ledger have died from overdoses involving opioids.

The opioid epidemic is certainly making profits for the makers of prescription painkillers and addiction is perhaps preferable to people rioting or carrying out rape or murder. However, the scale of the problem is a drag on the economy, since addicts aren't able to work or care for families and the USA has experienced a drop in life expectancy as a result, so Functionalists recognise it is **dysfunctional**. From a **Marxist** perspective, this is Big Pharma (the Capitalist medical industry) killing people to make money.

Research: find out more about the Opioid Epidemic, Big Pharma and the global trade in heroin and fentanyl

Opioid Epidemic (image by DES Daughter)

PERSPECTIVES ON CRIME & DEVIANCE

Perspectives are very broad viewpoints. They match the *"theoretical views"* the OCR Exam Board will assess you on. They are also important for evaluating **definitions and measures of crime and deviance** (p6) as well as how **patterns and trends** are interpreted (p26).

CONSENSUS PERSPECTIVE: FUNCTIONALISM

Functionalists usually take a **positive view** of crime and deviance. They regard crime as inevitable in all societies, partly because they acknowledge the role of human biology in shaping culture (and we are biologically evolved to be competitive and aggressive) and partly because, as **Durkheim's 'society of saints'** illustrates (p12), even highly moral communities will need to set boundaries on what is acceptable and therefore create the possibility of deviance. Durkheim adds that *"crime brings together upright consciences"* – by sharing our outrage at crime and pity for its victims, we reaffirm our culture's norms and values.

Crime is also important for **boundary maintenance**. People need to know what the boundaries of acceptable behaviour are and what will happen if they cross them. Therefore, it is important that, every now and again, someone transgresses by crossing a boundary and the rest of the community see what the consequences are. That way, they are reassured that the boundaries matter. Otherwise, the importance of boundaries fades and people experience **anomie**, which is a state of meaninglessness and detachment from society. Anomie can drive people to suicide and drug-abuse (such as the **American Opioid Epidemic**, p46) and also to rioting and violence.

Functionalism is a **structuralist** Perspective, so the (bad) impact of crime on individuals is not as important as its overall impact on society, which is often good. This is like the old proverb, 'In order to make an omelette, you have to break a few eggs.' Many people find this view rather callous and as society becomes more **individualistic** (perhaps due to **Postmodernity**, *c.f.* **3A: Globalisation & the Digital Social World**) it becomes a less convincing position for many people.

For Functionalists, individuals only behave well if they are **socialised** by a supportive family and community. If people feel detached from society, they have no motivation to behave well. People also weigh up their decisions rationally, taking into account **risks and rewards**. Therefore, people will commit crime if they feel they can get away with it, if the punishments are not unpleasant or if they feel unobserved or that nobody will judge them badly.

This means that Functionalist views on **preventing crime** (p65) focus on tough policing, strict punishments and creating communities where people are observed by their neighbours. They particularly like the idea of communities policing themselves (e.g. electing their own sheriffs in the USA or local police commissioners in the UK).

RESEARCH PROFILE: MERTON (1938)

Robert K Merton (1910-2003) was an American **Functionalist** who explained the rising crime in Chicago in the 1930s by using Durkheim's idea of **anomie** to create **Strain Theory**.

Merton suggests that every society has **cultural goals** that people are **socialised** into striving for. There are **institutionalised means** of reaching those goals. In the USA, this is the 'American Dream' of getting qualifications and working hard to become successful and independent (a form of **meritocracy**). **Strain** occurs when not everybody has the resources needed to reach this goal (e.g. poor education, no job opportunities). People adapt to this strain in five ways:

Conformity: persevere with the institutionalised means to reach the cultural goals (e.g. study harder, work more hours)

Innovation: use unconventional means to reach the cultural goals (e.g. become a drug dealer or rob a bank)

Ritualism: persevere with the institutionalised means but abandon the cultural goals (e.g. plug away at a dead-end job or choose more modest goals for yourself)

Retreatism: abandon the institutionalised means **and** the cultural goals (e.g. drop out, become a homeless person or a drug addict or just live on benefits watching TV all day)

Rebellion: work to replace the institutionalised means and cultural goals with new ones (e.g. become a political activist, a religious radical or a terrorist)

Robert K. Merton's Deviance Typology

Merton uses **official statistics** (p16) to develop Strain Theory and assumes that working class people commit crime to overcome the barriers placed in their way by an unfair society. However, he ignores **white collar crime** (why would already-successful people not conform?) and doesn't explain why most working class people remain law-abiding. His theory doesn't really explain violent crime or vandalism (**non-utilitarian crimes** that don't make you any richer).

Marxists would suggest that many criminals **internalise** the cultural goals, believing that they are only worthy of respect if they get rich (e.g. **Jock Young**'s concept of **social bulimia**, p53).

Subcultural Theories

Merton (like most Functionalists) assumes there is a **value consensus** about how to live which people only break with due to **anomie**. However, **Subcultural Theories** suggest that there might be **subcultures** in society with different value systems. Joining a **Criminal Subculture** and accepting its antisocial values would predispose you to committing crime.

Albert Cohen (1955, not the same Cohen who studied moral panics) suggests that working class boys experience **status frustration** when they cannot 'keep up' with middle class peers. They respond by joining an **Anti-School Subculture** where the values are inverted (flipped): it is bad to work hard and be praised by teachers, but good to cause trouble in class and get punished. Later, this subculture leads them into criminal behaviour too.

Cohen doesn't explain why most working class boys carry on working hard at school. His theory doesn't explain girls and only covers **delinquency** in the teenage years, not adult criminality.

The biggest problem with Subcultural Theories is that they abandon a central premise of Functionalism: that there is value consensus in society. Merton suggests that criminals still have the same *goals* as law-abiding people, just different *means* of reaching them. But Cohen seems to suggest that anti-school working class boys become something whole 'other': lifelong deviants who view society from a completely topsy-turvy moral basis. This is closer to **Conflict Theory**, which argues that the interests and goals of the working class are completely at odds with the ruling class and only the brainwashing power of **ideology** makes them think the same.

RESEARCH PROFILE: CLOWARD & OHLIN (1960)

Cloward & Ohlin argue that, alongside the **legitimate opportunity structure** (school, jobs, careers – the **meritocracy**), there is an **illegitimate opportunity structure** (a career in crime). Just as not all people can access the legitimate opportunity structure (because of poor qualifications, unemployment, etc.), the illegitimate opportunity structures aren't available to everyone either.

Cloward & Ohlin identify three illegitimate opportunity structures: **(1) Criminal**, which is organised, like the **Mafia** (pX), with a 'career path' for young recruits that mirrors the legitimate meritocratic structures (bonuses for good work, promotions, etc.); **(2) Conflict**, where gangs compete over territory ("turf wars"), which is violent and only occasionally lucrative (some money from drugs or theft); **(3) Retreatist**, where groups who cannot join organised crime or gangs simply 'drop out' and become drug addicts.

Hobbs & Dunningham (1998, p39) criticise the idea that the Mafia are still dominant in **global organised crime**. Instead, there is a **'glocal'** network where the boundary between organised criminals and gangs blur. Cloward & Ohlin don't explore *why* working class males are denied access to legitimate opportunities or why only a minority of working class males actually join these illegitimate opportunity structures instead. They don't explain why women, who are also denied opportunities, aren't more involved in crime.

The New Right

The New Right could be considered a 'spin-off' from Functionalism in the 1980s. Its central assumption is that the vital **value consensus** has collapsed so emergency measures are needed to restore it. The New Right diagnoses the core institution for value consensus as the **nuclear family** (married parents and their children) and the biggest threat to this as the **Welfare State**. The Welfare State is the political arrangement that pays benefits to the poor and the unemployed.

Critics of the Welfare State argue it **rewards worklessness** and **undermines the family** (since couples are not forced to stay together for monetary reasons if the state pays for their children).The single parent family (especially the single mother with children) is a target for the New Right, who argue that single parents cannot effectively **socialise** their children, who grow up 'feral': the girls get pregnant without marrying and live on child benefits, repeating the cycle, while the boys search for a father-figure and join gangs.

The New Right identifies a **'benefits trap'** that means unemployed people would end up worse off if they took a job, creating an incentive to stay unemployed and leading to **generational unemployment**, where families have parents and grandparents who do not work and claim benefits. The solution is to cut back benefits, forcing health adults to find work and take responsibility for their families.

*These are controversial arguments. Many people (including, but not limited to, **Marxists**) would argue that unemployed people desperately want to work and the stereotype of a chaotic and immoral families on benefits is a news media stereotype (see the case of **Shannon Matthews**, p31).*

Research: revisit your notes on **1A; Socialisation, Culture & Identity** and link these ideas to **social control in the workforce** – including the arguments by the **Joseph Rowntree Foundation (2012)** and **Macmillan (2011)** that cast doubt on the existence of the Underclass.

The New Right could be seen as a variation of **Subcultural Theory**, proposing just a single subculture, the Underclass, as responsible for society's problems. It 'others' the Underclass, demonising them as feral and antisocial, and this breaks away from the Functionalist idea of value consensus.

The New Right is condemned by **Marxists**, especially **Left Realists** (p56), for blaming crime on the very people who are most likely to be victims of it. Marxists object to the idea that poor people choose to live in poverty and lack a basic sense of right and wrong. **Jock Young (2003)** calls it a *"sociology of vindictiveness"* that tries to *"punish, demean and humiliate"* the poor.

Feminists criticise the New Right for demonising single mothers. Many Feminists regard it as an achievement to be celebrated that women can get away from abusive male partners and they do not support policies that would force unhappy couples to stay together or make mothers financially dependent on a man's earnings.

RESEARCH PROFILE: MURRAY (1984, 1989, 1999)

Charles Murray wrote the influential book *Losing Ground* **(1984)** which is the key statement of New Right thinking. Murray traces the rise of crime in the USA since the 1960s and finds it does not match trends in unemployment; however, it does match the trend for children born outside of marriage. Murray assumes a causal connection, with boys born to unmarried mothers growing up to be *"essentially barbarians."* A key assumption in Murray's thought is **that males are only civilised by marriage** and without the pressure to marry (which the Welfare State removes) they turn to drugs and crime. This is how the **Underclass** is created.

In 1989, Murray visited the UK and wrote an article for *The Sunday Times* in which he argued that Britain has a *"nascent* (meaning 'only just born') *Underclass."* Ten years later he followed up the research and concluded that the UK Underclass had become the same as the American one, just as he had previously warned: young males dropping out of the workforce, births to unmarried mothers rising, violent crime rising.

Murray's argument rests on a **statistical correlation** (worklessness, violent crime, illegitimate births) but correlations never prove cause-and-effect. Moreover, his ideas do not explain the **Great Crime Decline** (p24) but they are supported by research into the social backgrounds of violent offenders (p30).

Melanie Phillips (1999) is a **Right Realist** (p51) who argues that most of the problems Murray complains about originate in the upper classes, who started the trend for divorce and cohabitation (living together without marrying) and drug-taking before these habits spread to the working classes, saying *"that culture was created by our élites."* Phillips argues we must restore incentives for people to marry, not punish vulnerable people who make mistakes.

Right Realism

Another Perspective to emerge in the 1980s was **Realism**. Realists jettison the highly theoretical aspects of Consensus and Conflict Theory and focus on the more practical elements. **Right Realism** takes basic Functionalist ideas, but abandons concepts like value consensus, boundary maintenance and anomie. However, it keeps the focus on **individual responsibility**, the importance of **socialisation** and the insight that **people will behave badly unless society gives them a reason not to**.

Cornish & Clarke (1986) propose a **Rational Choice Theory** of crime. They claim that individuals engage in crime when opportunities present themselves and there seems to be little risk (a lack of **social control**, p6). Cornish & Clarke believe that criminals make rational decisions when deciding when to commit a crime or not. They cite burglary as an example: burglars ask themselves questions like, *Which house offers the best target? Do the neighbours watch out for each other? How hard will it be to gain entrance? What sorts of goods are inside? How will I get out in a hurry? What chance of success do I have?*

This means crime can be prevented by 'hardening' targets (p65), increasing the likelihood of being caught or increasing the severity of punishment to make the crime not worth the risk.

Right Realism is very similar to the **New Right** (p50) in its attitudes and many Right Realists accept Murray's concept of the **Underclass**. However, Right Realists believe crime needs to be solved by more practical methods than cutting benefits or penalising single parent families.

RESEARCH PROFILE: WILSON (1975)

James Q Wilson (1975) pioneered the Right Realist approach in his book *Thinking About Crime* *(1975)*. Wilson takes the view that factors like family structure, unemployment and cultural attitudes to marriage are impossible to control, so it's not worth focusing on them. He points out that most poor people are law-abiding so poverty cannot be the cause of crime.

Wilson claims that crime is linked to a breakdown in **social order** (p6). Disorder in neighbourhoods causes a loss of a sense of community, a decline in **informal social control** and this breeds crime. Wilson believes that architecture affects the way people behave: if you are surrounded by damaged and run-down buildings, you see this as an excuse to commit crime.

This means crime can be prevented by improving the physical environment of our cities: removing graffiti and litter and challenging those who produce it as well as designing streets and buildings to encourage neighbours to feel a sense of community.

Wilson also argues that crime is reduced by enforcing the law (similar to the **Rational Choice Theory** of crime, p51). However, Wilson argues that severe punishments aren't as important as the **certainty of detection**: if punishments are severe but the likelihood of being caught is low, offenders will gamble on getting away with it; if the likelihood of being caught is high, offenders will be deterred even if the punishments are mild.

Research: revisit your notes on **1A; Socialisation, Culture & Identity** and link these ideas to **Wilson & Kelling**'s idea of '**Broken Windows**' and **Zero Tolerance Policing:** can you see now why these are Right Realist ideas? And yes, the 'Wilson' of Wilson & Kelling is **James Q Wilson**.

AO2 ILLUSTRATION: THE COLUMBINE SCHOOL SHOOTINGS

In 1999, **Eric Harris and Dylan Klebold**, two American teenagers, went into **Columbine High School, Colorado** armed with shotguns and home-made bombs. They killed 13 people (12 of their fellow students and one teacher) and wounded 20 more and would have harmed more people if their bombs had gone off successfully. Both gunmen shot themselves after the police arrived.

Harris and Klebold were considered outsiders by their peers because of their **Goth** fashion (wearing long black trench coats). They left behind homemade videotapes in which they showed their plans, methods and practising with guns. The pair had a love for violent video games (e.g. *Doom*) and gloomy rock music (e.g. Marilyn Manson) and an obsession with death and guns that appeared in their school work. They came from conventional and loving families.

Consensus sociologists find a lot of support in mass shootings like this, where the killers are isolated misfits who are not integrated into society and suffer from **anomie**. The fact that they belong to a violent subculture hostile to society is significant too. However, Harris and Klebold were not from the **Underclass**; they were products of exactly the sort of healthy nuclear families that **Functionalists** and the **New Right** endorse. They carried out their attacks while being recorded by CCTV cameras, which is a problem for the **Right Realist** view.

Research: find out about other school shootings and relate them to Consensus theories; watch Michael Moore's documentary *Bowling For Columbine* (2002)

CONFLICT PERSPECTIVE: MARXISM

Marxists don't accept that crime comes from being badly socialised and they certainly don't agree that there's something inherently deviant about being working class.

Instead, Marxists argue that Capitalism itself is **criminogenic** – it is a system that creates crime and drives people to commit crime. **Young (1984)** claims we live in a 'bulimic society' where the constant need to get the latest products, brands and fashions causes people to become deranged.

For Marxists, the real criminals are the rulers of the Capitalist system and they argue that the **White Collar Crime** carried out by corporations does far more damage to society than muggers or hooligans on the streets.

However, **ruling class ideology** (especially as it is presented through the **Media**) causes people to focus on the wrong things. People have an exaggerated fear of street crime and working class youths, but dismiss white collar crime as harmless or unimportant. The police crack down on working class youths, but don't pursue white collar criminals; this is called **selective enforcement**.

This can be explained by **Althusser (1970)** who identifies the **Ideological State Apparatus** (**ISA**, e.g. the Media) and the **Repressive State Apparatus** (**RSA**, e.g. the police) which combine to support Capitalism.

Research: revisit your notes on **1A: Socialisation, Culture & Identity** and link these ideas to **Jock Young**, **Edwin Sutherland** and **Louis Althusser**.

Traditional Marxists are sceptical about working class crime and in the past tended to dismiss it as a fiction created by the news media to justify the use of the police and demonise the working classes. Over time, this view has become less credible and most Marxists today accept that working class crime is real, but they tend to insist that the **white collar crimes** of the wealthy are just as important or more so.

RESEARCH PROFILE: GORDON (1971)

David M Gordon (1971) wrote *Class & the Economics of Crime* **(1971)** in which he says that Capitalist societies are "*dog eat dog societies*" in which each individual is encouraged to look out for their own interests before anyone else's, including the wider community and the environment. Capitalism encourages us to be greedy and teaches us that it is acceptable to harm others in pursuit of our selfish desires. This is the basis of crime.

Gordon argues that the police focus attention on working class areas and the criminal justice system (CJS) focuses on prosecuting working class criminals. The CJS ignores the crimes of the wealthy, although they are just as likely (or more) to commit crime as the working classes.

Selective law enforcement (p21) benefits the Capitalist system in three major ways: (**1**) by punishing individuals and making an example of them as '*social failures*' it covers up the flaws in society (inequality and poverty) that create the conditions which lead to crime; (**2**) oppressing the working classes neutralises the only people motivated to resist ruling class dominance; (**3**) imprisoning criminals hides away "*worst jetsam of Capitalist society*" so the rest of us do not see the real human cost of Capitalism.

Gordon's ideas are echoed by **Holdaway**'s study of police occupational culture (p17) and **Jock Young**'s concept of **social bulimia** (p53).

Neo-Marxism / Radical Criminology

Neo means 'new' and **Neo-Marxism** emerged in the 1970s as update of Marxist thought. A big inspiration was **Antonio Gramsci (1891-1937)** who moved away from the idea of a revolution to overthrow Capitalism. Gramsci observed that the ruling class was no longer a literal class of aristocrats and factory owners, but had become a **Hegemony**, a confederation of influential people with a vested interest in keeping Capitalism going. Gramsci pointed out that Hegemony **'manufactures consent'** through education and the Media.

Neo-Marxists take the basic Marxist idea that Capitalism is **criminogenic** and the laws are **selectively enforced** to benefit the ruling class, but they add insights from **Interactionism** (especially **Labelling Theory**, p13) that the rulers have the power to **label marginalised groups** as deviant and that people can **internalise** this label, viewing themselves that way (the **Self-Fulfilling Prophecy**).

Neo-Marxists therefore recognise that working class people do in fact commit crime – the **official crime statistics** (p16) do describe something real. However, for Neo-Marxists it is important to understand *why* working class crime occurs. It is a form of **resistance** to Capitalism. Resistance falls short of revolution. Crime is not an attempt to overthrow Capitalism, but it is a **symbolic** statement of opposition and non-consent to hegemonic values. It is a way for working class people to protest the system and the inequalities in their lives.

This comes very close to a **Functionalist** argument, that crime is a way of venting frustration and signalling dysfunction. However, Neo-Marxists argue crime needs to be understood as a symbol or a ritual; it is not just a protest demanding more rights or more money but rather it is a coded way of wishing to dismantle the entire Capitalist system.

Meanwhile, Neo-Marxists continue to assert that the **white collar crime** of the ruling class is far more damaging than the petty street crime of the working classes and that the police and the news media combine to focus on working class crime, almost to the exclusion of anything else. Neo-Marxist arguments like this appear in **Hall**'s *Policing The Crisis* (p27).

RESEARCH PROFILE: TAYLOR, WALTON & YOUNG (1972)

Ian Taylor, Paul Walton & Jock Young (yes, him again!) wrote *The New Criminology* (1972) in which they present a *"radical theory of crime"* – hence their approach is sometimes called **radical criminology** (and appears as this in the OCR Specification, so make sure you revise this bit!) but you will also see it called **critical criminology**.

They argue for a *"fully social theory of deviance"* which considers the way a Capitalist society is structured (just like any Marxist criminology) but also the motives of the individuals involved (that's the *"radical"* bit). They don't just mean the motives of the offenders (that would be what **Subcultural Theory** already does) but also the motives of the police and judges involved.

Radical Criminology focuses on three aspects of a crime: (**1**) the **circumstances** surrounding the choice to commit the crime (e.g. poverty, discrimination, lack of education – standard Marxist focus on inequality); (**2**) the **meaning of the act** for the individual; (**3**) the **societal reaction**, including **labelling** and **deviancy amplification** (based on **Interactionism**, p59).

Radical Criminologists contend that the *meaning of the act* is not usually to gain money or hurt someone; rather it is to resist Capitalism: it is meant to be a symbolic act of defiance.

Critics of Radical Criminology point out that very few crimes have a clear political meaning to them; most are much more straightforwardly about getting money or settling scores. However, unlike **Strain Theory** (p48), Radical Criminology is quite good at explaining **non-utilitarian** crime, like violence, arson, vandalism and graffiti. **Left Realists** (including Jock Young himself, a decade later) criticise Radical Criminology for painting working class criminals as 'Robin Hood' figures and ignoring the harm they do to their (usually working class) victims.

Left Realism

Right Realism emerged in the 1980s but another Realist Perspective emerged to answer it: **Left Realism**. Left Realists jettison the highly theoretical aspects of Conflict Theory and focus on the more practical elements. **Left Realism** takes basic Marxist ideas but abandons concepts like resistance to Capitalism (which was so important for **Neo Marxism**, p54). However, it keeps the focus on **Capitalism being criminogenic**, the importance of **selective policing** and the insight that **people will behave well unless society gives them a reason not to**.

Jock Young (1986) terms the earlier types of Marxist criminologists (including his own **radical criminology**) as 'Left Idealists.' He argues that Left Realists must steer a path between two extremes: on the one hand the **New Right** who are hysterical about the **Underclass** (p50) and want to over-police marginalised communities; on the other hand the Left Idealists who are in denial about the negative impact of crime on the most vulnerable people in society.

For example, the **Islington Crime Survey** (p19) was crucial in supporting the Left Realist view, because it showed people in a very deprived neighbourhood – especially women – suffering a 'curfew' because of the realistic fear of crime.

Left Realism involves being tough on crime, but also tough on the causes of crime. It's a two-pronged approach, which involves using the police to detect and punish criminals, but making sure they police communities fairly, and also alleviating the poverty and inequality that makes crime attractive for people in those communities.

By acknowledging working class criminality, Left Realism could be criticised for abandoning the strict defence of the working class of earlier Marxism and giving credibility to moral panics in the news media. However, it has been immensely influential, especially in the Labour Government of 1997-2010, and has had more political results than any other type of Marxist criminology.

RESEARCH PROFILE: LEA & YOUNG (1984)

John Lea & Jock Young (again!) wrote *What's To Be Done About Law & Order?* (1984) in which they make the case for Left Realism. There are three key concepts: **relative deprivation**, **marginalisation** and **subculture**.

Lea & Young argue that crime is caused by deprivation, but deprivation itself is not directly responsible for crime; they admit that deprivation has fallen since the austerity of the 1950s but crime has gone up. **Relative deprivation** refers to how someone feels compared to other people or their own expectations. Although people are better off today, they have a feeling of relative deprivation because advertising has raised expectations for material possessions – we are wealthier, but we feel poorer. This creates a pressure to keep up with expectations, which leads to crime. This idea influenced **Jock Young**'s theory of **social bulimia** (p53).

Marginalisation is where people cannot participate fully in society. Marginalised groups lack organisations to represent their interests and clear goals. For example, workers have groups to represent them (e.g. trade unions) and clear goals (e.g. better pay) so they don't need to resort to crime. Marginalised groups (e.g. the unemployed or youth) have no clear goals and no one representing them, so they turn to crime in frustration.

A group's collective response to relative deprivation and marginalisation is to form a **subculture** – this is similar to **Cohen's theory of status frustration** (p49). There are **subcultural adaptations** to the problems that groups face and not all involve crime (e.g. some marginalised groups become very religious). However, some subcultures retain the mainstream cultural goal of acquiring wealth but lack the resources to achieve it and these are at risk of becoming criminal subcultures – this is similar to **Merton's Strain Theory** (p48).

Lea & Young argue that crime is caused by lots of different factors (termed a **multiple aetiology**) so it is important to understand why people offend, what shapes public attitudes and responses to crime and the factors that influence the police. They propose that an effective community should work *together* to solve crime.

AO2 ILLUSTRATION: THE MACPHERSON REPORT (1999)

Four years after the murder of **Stephen Lawrence** in 1993 (p35), a Government Inquiry was set up to look into the way the Metropolitan Police had handled the case. Sir William Macpherson chaired the investigation, and the **'Stephen Lawrence Inquiry'** is known as the **Macpherson Report**, which was published in 1999. It ran to 350 pages and contained 70 recommendations. Macpherson concluded that the police investigation into Stephen Lawrence's death had been *"marred by a combination of professional incompetence, institutional racism and a failure of leadership"* Officers in the Metropolitan police were named and shamed and the entire force was criticised.

Following the report, the Metropolitan Police introduced targets to recruit and promote Black and Asian officers and the **Independent Police Complaints Commission** was set up to monitor the police.

Macpherson defined **institutional racism** as *"the collective failure of an organisation to provide an appropriate and professional service to people because of their colour, culture or ethnic origin."* The point about institutional racism is that it is based on the way an organisation works, so the individuals in it might not be personally racist, but they will act as if they were just by following the organisation's rules and procedures.

The Macpherson Report is strong support for **Neo-Marxist** and **Left Realist** ideas about **selective policing** (p21); it backs up the findings of **Holdaway** (p17) and **Fitzgerald's Policing For London Survey** (p35) and continues to inform the debate about **Stop & Search** targeting Black people.

CONFLICT PERSPECTIVE: FEMINISM

Feminists don't offer an explanation of all crime everywhere. Instead, they challenge stereotypes about women and draw attention to crimes committed against women and the unfair way they are treated by the criminal justice system (CJS).

For example, the **Chivalry Thesis** (p32) claims that women are treated better by the CJS, which is why there are fewer arrests or convictions for women. On the face of it, this is supported by **self-report studies** (p20) that show offending rates for males and females are much closer than the huge gulf found in **official crime statistics** (p16). **Frances Heidensohn (1985)** explains it is more complex than this: women who show conventionally feminine behaviour (crying, showing love for their children) may be treated leniently, but those who do not conform to expectations of femininity are treated more harshly.

When it comes to victimisation, **Sandra Walklate (1995)** found female rape victims face a tough rather than chivalrous court system; women who are raped are often not believed and have to prove their respectability before their accusation is taken seriously.

Adler's Liberation Thesis (p33) predicts more women will get involved in crime and this might be proved by the emergence of a **'Ladette' Subculture** in the 1990s and 2000s. However, most Feminists contend that women's crimes are driven, not by liberation, but by poverty and oppression, for example **prostitution** (which is the *only* crime where females outnumber males).

Prostitution and sex work have created a division in Feminism. The **2nd Wave Feminists** of the 1960s and '70s viewed prostitution as exploitation of women by men and many Feminists continue to view it this way. The **4th Wave Feminists** of the 21st century adopt a more **sex-positive** view, arguing that the real problem is that attitude of shame and judgement about women's bodies. Feminists like **Priscilla Alexander (1997)** argue that **sex work** (they do not call it 'prostitution') can be liberating for women and instead of being driven underground it should be legalised, regulated and made safe. The term **'whorephobic'** is sometimes used to attack Feminists who oppose sex work. However, **Julie Bindel (2017)** describes prostitution as *"paid rape"* saying *"if 'consent' has to be bought, it is not consent."*

Sex Work Is Work (photo: SG ZA)

RESEARCH PROFILE: SMART (1976)

Carol Smart wrote *Women, Crime & Criminology* (1976) which had a big impact on the up-till-that-point male world of criminology. She explains that women remain *"invisible"* in male-dominated criminology, and particularly their victimisation is ignored.

Smart suggests that biological differences between sexes aren't an important factor in the cause of crime causing crime. She argues that there is stricter **socialisation** of girls than boys within the family. Parents control how often girls go out, where to and with whom. Girls learn to share exaggerated fears about their safety, even though stranger attacks are rare and boys are far more likely to be victims of violence. This leads to girls and later women becoming prisoners in their own homes.

Women offenders are perceived as **doubly deviant** because they not only break the law but also transgress their gender role, which is to be subordinate and obedient. This is the *opposite* of the **Chivalry Thesis**, but it ties in with **Heidensohn**'s point about women who fail to conform to gender expectations being treated more harshly.

SOCIAL ACTION PERSPECTIVE: INTERACTIONISM

Interactionists reject the sort of structuralist explanations presented so far, like the idea that entire classes of people are behaving a certain way because of social forces.

This approach uses the idea of **societal reaction**. Society (with the help of the news media) picks on a few unconnected cases of people behaving in a deviant way. These cases really have nothing to do with each other, but the media pulls them together in an **ideological framework** (an 'explanation that makes sense'), giving the phenomenon a title like 'crime wave.' All the people involved in it that are now labelled 'criminals.'

Edwin Lemert (1967) points out a distinction between **primary and secondary deviance**.

Primary deviance is something everybody does: we've all stolen things (if only pens from the office or towels from the hotel), broken the law, damaged things that don't belonged to us, had romantic interactions with someone we shouldn't, used obscene language or been violent. Most of the time it goes unnoticed and there are no consequences.

Secondary deviance is deviance that society reacts to. Someone 'calls it out' and assigns a label: we are blamed, accused; people are shocked; the authorities step in. This includes being labelled as a criminal (or a 'thug' or a a 'slut'). At first this label doesn't conform to our self-image and that leads to anxiety. Eventually, we alter our self-image to conform to the label: this is the **Self-Fulfilling Prophecy (SFP)**.

Some labels have **Master Status** and are particularly hard to negotiate or remove. If you are labelled as 'lazy' you can negotiate that label (*'I'm only lazy with subjects I don't enjoy'*) or prove it wrong. If you are labelled as a criminal. It's hard to negotiate (it's no good saying you're not a criminal because you only steal from rich people) or remove – the label can stick for years. Since young people have less power in society, it's harder for them to avoid secondary deviance or negotiate deviant labels.

Howard Becker (1963) applies the idea of societal reaction to marijuana smokers. He argues that drug-users have to learn from others how to take a drug. When agencies of social control 'clamp down,' users start to see themselves as drug-users (rather than just friends with a similar pastime): they accept their **deviant label** and the drug becomes central to their lifestyle. In this way, attempts to prevent drug-use end up creating, rather than preventing, drug-addicts.

Research: revisit your notes on **1A: Socialisation, Culture & Identity** and link these ideas to **Howard Becker's** *Outsiders*

Critics say that secondary deviance is only a good explanation of delinquency and non-serious crime; it's hard to argue that murder is only regarded as criminal because society labels it that way. It's also hard to see how labelling can explain hidden crimes like child abuse.

Interactionism is accused of being a ***description*** of crime rather than an ***explanation***. For example, why does society single out certain individuals or groups in the first place? where does the ideological framework tying these behaviours together come from? why does the news media stir up outrage rather than, say, curiosity or admiration?

Neo-Marxists like **Stuart Hall** (**1978**, p27) claim to have the answer to this: the Media has a structural relationship to Capitalist institutions, so it regularly scapegoats marginalised groups to blame them for crises in Capitalism.

RESEARCH PROFILE: CHAMBLISS (1973)

In 1973, **William Chambliss** published *The Saints & the Roughnecks*, an article describing two years spent observing Hannibal High School students (age 16-19) in America. He followed two gangs: six working class Roughnecks and eight middle class Saints. (The names of the gangs and the school are fictional to protect the anonymity of the boys and their families).

Chambliss observed that the Saints' behaviour was in many ways *worse* than the Roughnecks, engaging in truancy, under-age drinking, dangerous driving and vandalism. Yet they were seen as model students, whereas the Roughnecks were constantly in trouble with teachers and police.

The Saints were successful in school, viewed as 'good students' by the teachers and found it easy to truant by pretending to have extracurricular activities. Since they had cars, they could travel to other suburbs or into the city to misbehave, where no one would recognise them. When they got into trouble with the police, they could pay fines and their parents would vouch for them.

The Roughnecks were viewed as delinquents. Their truancy was lower than the Saints, but it was public knowledge. Without cars, they had to gather in their own neighbourhood, where their fighting and drunkenness was observed. There were in trouble with the police and, while Chambliss observed them, each Roughneck was arrested at least once.

Chambliss uses **Labelling Theory** to explain his findings: the Saints had positive labels so their behaviour was interpreted as harmless; the Roughnecks were interpreted as delinquent because of their negative labels. The Saints went on to college and good jobs. The Roughnecks had different outcomes: attempted suicide, prison, gambling, unemployment.

Chambliss connects this to a **Marxist** understanding of class and privilege. Social control is imposed on the working classes, but not the middle classes, and this control *creates* deviancy rather than reducing it.

Chambliss' study is from the 1970s and the USA, so the results might not apply to 21st century criminals or the UK, where teenagers don't drive until they are 18 but they can legally buy alcohol before they are 21. The boys were white, so the study doesn't tell us about other ethnic groups or girls. The small sample size, although typical of **Interactionist** research, is hard to generalise from: these could have been unusual teenagers at an unusual school.

Chambliss is a **Neo-Marxist** *so his research could be used to support that Perspective (p54). The Saints' ability to negotiate with the police and avoid detection can be used to analyse* **social class patterns & trends** *(p30).*

Research: review your notes for **1A: Socialisation, Culture & Identity** to link this study to **Willis'** *Learning To Labour* **(1973)** where 'the Lads' behave similarly to Chambliss' Roughnecks (although they are a year or two younger). It is also interesting to compare with the Spur Posse observed by **Faludi** in *Stiffed* **(1991).**

AO2 ILLUSTRATION: ONLYFANS BANS PORN

OnlyFans (OF) is a subscriber website that features content creators offering recipes and yoga instruction but is mainly famous for porn. *OF* has tens of thousands of sex workers who hand over 20% of their earnings to the site – but in 2021 *OF* announced it would ban pornographic content. This led to sex workers on the site claiming it was destroying their livelihoods. Defenders argue that sex work online is safer for women and enables them to be their own bosses. Critics point out that women are scammed, stalked and trolled on the site and the site owners do not listen to the complaints of women who are abused by their 'fans.'

OF is a good example of the **debate about sex work within Feminism** (p58), but also the way in which female deviancy is treated differently from male deviancy (the idea of **relativity** and **social construction**) since *OF* is closing down businesses that are not actually illegal and which are largely carried out by women. The term 'sex worker' is an attempt to **negotiate a different label**, because 'prostitute' has **master status**.

EXAM PRACTICE: EXPLAINING CRIME & DEVIANCE

The OCR exam has three questions in **Paper 3 Section B**. Questions 7-9 are on Education and questions 10-12 are on Religion, Belief & Faith, but this Study Guide is focused on **Option 1** which covers questions **4-6**:

4. In what ways is does Feminism explain gender differences in offending? **[10 marks: 6 AO1 + 4 AO2]**

This is one of those 'describe & illustrate' questions, but with no Source A or Source B to lean on. No need to evaluate.

Make two sociological points about Feminism and gender differences –a point about male offending and a point about female offending. It's a good idea to refer to particular statistics (like 80% of crime being male) and you should definitely use some sociological terminology (like socialisation, the invisibility of women and the Chivalry Thesis). Then offer examples of crimes and make sure each example has an explanation. For example, "Females are more involved in crime than they were, such as the rise of Ladette culture."

5. To what extent is the New Right a good explanation of social class differences in offending? **[20 marks: 8 AO1 + 4 AO2 + 8 AO3]**

This is a mid-size essay with a requirement for developed evaluation. You should spend 25 minutes and write at least 500 words.

*Write **three** points. Each point should introduce a sociological idea with some illustration from the real world. Each point should finish off with a developed evaluation (see **Chapter 5** for this). For example, you could write about the benefits trap, single parent families and violent young males. Make sure you mention **Murray**'s research and be sure to answer the question: is the New Right a good explanation or not?*

6. Outline and evaluate radical criminology as an explanation of crime and deviance. **[40 marks: 16 AO1 + 8 AO2 + 16 AO3]**

This is the last of the two big (40 mark) essays in OCR A-Level Sociology. You should spend 50 minutes and write at least 1000 words.

*Write **five** points. Each point should introduce a sociological idea with some illustration from the real world. Each point should finish off with a developed evaluation (see **Chapter 5** for this). For example, you could write about Neo-Marxism being different from traditional Marxism, the importance of Interactionism, the idea of pre-crime circumstances, the motive for the act and post-crime labelling. Make a point of mentioning **Taylor et al**'s book **The New Criminology** but don't forget about **Hall** and **Chambliss** too. Be sure to come to a conclusion: is radical criminology the best explanation or was Left Realism a better replacement?*

CHAPTER FOUR – REDUCING CRIME & DEVIANCE

The OCR Specification asks '**How can crime and deviance be reduced?**' and it goes on to define "*reduced*" as **prevention**, **punishment** and **control**:

- **Prevention** means strategies that make crime and deviance less likely to occur in the first place. This includes punishments that are so frightening that people don't dare misbehave (**deterrence**) as well as things to make misbehaviour harder or less appealing.
- **Punishment** means strategies to respond to a crime after it has occurred. Punishment can make someone less likely to reoffend (**reformation**) because the punishment was so awful no one would want to go through it again. Punishment can be **retribution**, enforcing the values of the law-abiding community, or **reparation**, which is getting the offender to repair the damage they have caused.
- **Control** means changing people so that they don't misbehave in future. It can involve rehabilitating offenders to make them into better citizens or just monitoring them closely, so they find it more difficult to re-offend (**protection** of the public).

These strategies are part of **social policy**, which means the actions taken by the police, the courts, social services (like youth workers) and laws passed by the government to reduce crime and deviance.

Because social policy involves politics, you need to understand an important political distinction.

Right Wing politics

Right Wing politics are inspired by **Consensus Theory** in sociology and are represented in the UK by the **Conservative Party**. Right Wing views favour traditional institutions (family, church, the Royal Family) and tend to be nationalistic. They prefer gradual reform and are suspicious of revolutionary change. They prefer power to be located close to communities (e.g. at a town council or parish level) and are suspicious of 'Big Government' and giving more power to the state – and especially to international organisations like the EU and UN. Right Wingers value marriage and work and are suspicious of benefits and anything that seems to reward laziness or irresponsibility.

Right Wing Views on Crime Reduction

It is a Right Wing idea that **people will behave badly unless society gives them a reason not to**. This means humans will be violent, selfish and criminal unless something restrains them from behaving that way – and what restrains them is **social order** (p6), which means pressure from their family and community and an awareness of the risks of breaking the rules. People are individually responsible for their crimes and you can't shift the blame to poverty, inequality or the structure of society.

On a society-wide level, crime is best reduced by making sure people are in work and living as part of a healthy family unit. Young men in particular need to be socialised by discipline from parents and later by responsibilities in a marriage. Strong communities keep crime in check.

On a more local level, people need to be watched. The anonymity of living in a big city encourages crime but having architecture that lets neighbours see what's going on and gives troublemakers nowhere to hide reduces this problem.

People are rational when it comes to crime, so if you make the risks outweigh the benefits crime will reduce. This means tough punishments for crime and visible police presence – or else CCTV cameras that assure people they won't get away with crime.

Left Wing politics

Left Wing politics are inspired by **Conflict Theory** in sociology and are represented in the UK by the **Labour Party** and the **Green Party** and (to a lesser extent) the **Liberal Democrats**. Left Wing views regard traditional institutions as unhelpful and out-of-date; they tend to be international in outlook and suspicious of nationalism. They prefer sweeping changes over gradual reform. They regard 'Big Government' as a powerful ally in bringing about social change. Left Wingers are concerned for the marginalised people in society – the poor, ethnic minority groups, LGBT minorities, etc. – and believe the majority should make sacrifices to benefit these minorities, such as taxing the wealthy to fund the Welfare State.

Left Wing Views on Crime Reduction

It is a Left Wing idea that **people will behave well unless society gives them a reason not to**. This means humans will only be violent, selfish and criminal if society forces them to behave this way – and what forces them to do this is poverty, discrimination and frustration at being excluded. People are not necessarily individually responsible for their crimes and you can't blame the criminal without taking into account the circumstances that produced him or her.

On a society-wide level, crime is best reduced by making sure people are more equal and fully included in society. Discrimination based on race, gender, religion or background needs to be challenged. More money needs to be spent benefiting deprived communities.

On a more local level, people need to be consulted. The police need to work *with* local communities, not *against* them, and the makeup of the police force should match the demographics of the society they police (e.g. in terms of ethnicity).

Criminals are in some sense victims too, so being tough on them only brutalises them and makes them more hostile. Sentences need to focus on rehabilitating people so they can rejoin society and play a constructive role in future.

Research: revisit your notes on **3A: Globalisation & the Digital Social World** and combine these ideas with the details about the Culture Wars and Social Justice – and in **1A: Socialisation, Culture & Identity** you can link this to the debate over Defunding The Police.

REDUCING CRIME & DEVIANCE: A TOOLKIT

The OCR Specification expects you to be able to discuss Right Wing and Left Wing approaches to reducing crime in detail. These approaches are:

Left Wing	Right Wing
Community crime prevention & punishment	Situational & environmental crime prevention
Restorative Justice	Retributive justice
Structural changes in society	Punitive punishment & control

We will consider Right Wing approaches first as they are more representative of the political approach in the UK today and over the last decade or more.

SITUATIONAL & ENVIRONMENTAL CRIME PREVENTION

Ronald Clarke (1983) discusses five aspects of crime prevention: (**1**) **increase effort** of crime, such as using locks, screens and barriers between the criminal and their target; (**2**) **increase risk** of being caught, including street lighting, security guards and Neighbourhood Watch schemes; (**3**) **reduce rewards** of crime by hiding valuable goods, moving away from cash and fitting ink tags that ruin stolen goods; (**4**) **reduce provocations**, such as segregating hostile fans at sports matches, reducing crowding in pubs and banning violent pornography; (**5**) **remove excuses** by making the rules clear, such as through obvious signs ('No Parking') and roadside displays that inform motorists of their speed.

Situational crime prevention is also known as **target hardening**. It involves making crime more difficulty, inconvenient or risky in specific situations. Classic examples are burglar alarms on houses and central locking on cars, PINs on mobile phones and electromagnetic tags on shop goods like clothes or alcohol (those plastic clips the shop assistant removes when you buy them and set off an alarm if you leave with them).

If criminals are rational, these strategies make crime a less attractive choice: **effort is increased** and **rewards are reduced**. They are also mostly used by businesses or private individuals, so they don't involve extending the reach of Big Government into people's private lives, which is good from a Right Wing viewpoint.

Environmental crime prevention is about making sure an entire area (like a tower block, an estate or a city street) is constructed in a way that deters crime. This includes things like street lighting and designing homes to give neighbours a view outside their property so they see people coming and going. This **increases risk** and **reduces provocation and excuses**.

Clarke includes **surveillance** in this category, particularly CCTV cameras. Right Wing critics are less keen on CCTV, since it infringes on individual privacy.

AO2 ILLUSTRATION: FACIAL RECOGNITION TECHNOLOGY

There are at least 5 million CCTV cameras in the UK, which is one for every 13 people – however 96% are owned by householders or businesses and only 4% are owned by the state (source: **CCTV.co.uk**).

New **automatic facial recognition (AFR)** technology allows such cameras to access databases and identify people walking or driving past. China has invested heavily in AFR, but there is opposition in Western countries, based on civil liberties and the right to privacy.

In 2020, the UK Court of Appeal ruled that South Wales Police's use of AFR was *"unlawful"* and the EU is considering banning AFR in public places.

Police forces must have a reason to use this technology (rather than just 'fishing' through public places) and a human officer must double-check identifications made (since the technology is alleged to be biased towards identifying White faces accurately).

RESEARCH PROFILE: NEWMAN (1972)

City planner **Oscar Newman** wrote *Defensible Space* **(1972)** in which he argues that architecture can reduce crime. Newman studies a New York tower block and a low-rise estate with similar levels of deprivation but found crime was higher in the tower block, where residents could not look out onto their own gardens or monitor who was coming or going in the building. In particular, gangs vandalised the lifts and occupied the stairwells where they were out of sight but could menace passers-by.

Newman defines defensible space as *"a residential environment whose physical characteristics – building layout and site plan – function to allow inhabitants themselves to become key agents in ensuring their security."* He argues that humans are naturally territorial and want to monitor their territory and make it secure. Housing should exploit this tendency for the mutual benefit of all the residents, so that people take responsibility for their surroundings.

Newman was an architect not a sociologist, but his ideas mirror the **Right Realist** (p51) focus on the importance of surveillance and the reduction of anonymity to prevent crime. However, his conclusions have been criticised because not all projects built according to his ideas have shown reduced crime and even when they do the reasons might be something other than territoriality (such as better jobs and opportunities around a new housing development).

RETRIBUTIVE JUSTICE

Retributive justice is the idea that the punishment should fit the crime and reflect the values of the community: the offender should experience the outrage of the entire community they have wronged, not just their specific victim. It is important for **boundary maintenance** (p6).

Retributive punishment tends to involve lengthy **custodial sentences** (meaning prison sentences) and it is proposed that this deters people from offending and causes prisoners to think twice about re-offending. However, with 47% of prisoners re-offending within a year of being released (source: **Prison Reform Trust, 2013**), this justification is contested. **Right Realists** maintain that the reason prison does not deter is because it is in fact too 'soft.'

Another argument for retributive justice is that it enables the offender to experience moral growth. 'Softer' punishments only delude convicts into thinking that their offence was not really so serious, which cheats them of self-knowledge and the opportunity to turn themselves around. Left Realist **John Braithwaite (1989)** called this **disintegrative shaming** and argues that **restorative justice** (p73) is what leads to personal change. The Interactionist **Howard Garfunkel (1956)** calls them **degradation ceremonies** and argues they apply negative labels to people.

The ultimate form of retributive justice is **capital punishment** (the death penalty). This is based on the idea that the value of a life in society can be measured by the punishment given to someone who takes a life, so execution is the only fair punishment for a murderer. The death penalty still exists in (as of 2021) 24 out of 50 US States but was abolished in the UK in 1965 (1973 in Northern Ireland). Of course, capital punishment does *not* permit an offender to grow in moral self-knowledge (unless there's an afterlife).

Not all **Right Realists** agree with retributive justice; **James Q Wilson** (p52) argues that certainty of being detected is much more effective at reducing crime than the harshness of the punishment.

AO2 ILLUSTRATION: THREE STRIKES & YOU'RE OUT

In 1994, the USA introduced **habitual offender laws**, which were nicknamed '**Three Strikes Laws**' based on the phrase used in baseball to describe a hitter being declared 'out' after three swings and misses. The laws (which vary from State to State) means that the third time a person is convicted of a serious crime, the judge has no choice but give a long custodial (prison) sentence.

An example is from 2009 when a Leonard Andrade stole $153 worth of videotapes from a K-Mart store. He had previous convictions for drugs and burglary so under California's 'Three Strikes Law' he was sentenced to 50 years in prison with no chance of parole.

This illustrates a fierce debate over 'Three Strikes Laws.' Defenders claim the punishment deters criminals and makes the rational choice to commit a third crime very risky. Critics point out that a 50 year sentence for stealing $153 is wildly disproportionate. 'Three Strikes' has been linked to the **McDonaldisation** of punishment (**Ritzer, 1993**) because it makes machine-like efficiency more important than making sure an offender gets the punishment he or she morally deserves.

RESEARCH PROFILE: BECKETT & EVANS (2018)

Katherine Beckett & Heather Evans produced a report on the role of race in capital sentencing for the Washington State Supreme Court in 2018. Based on their findings, the Court then voted to abolish the death penalty after 99 years of use.

Beckett & Evans studied all capital cases in the State from 1981-2014 and found that Black defendants were between 3.5 and 4.6 times more likely to receive a death sentence than non-Black defendants. They found that juries were more than 4 times likely to impose a death sentence for Black defendants. In counties with high Black populations, prosecutors were more likely to request the death penalty and judges to sentence convicted felons to death. The researchers explain this by **'implicit racial bias,'** a psychological term describing the same processes that the **Macpherson Report** terms **institutional racism** (p57). The researchers conclude that *"race-blindness continues to elude us."*

The study illustrates a problem with capital punishment: it is disproportionately applied to marginalised groups even when the police, lawyers and judges are not consciously racist.

PUNITIVE PUNISHMENT & CONTROL

*'Punitive' just means 'punishing' so 'punitive punishment' is a bit of a redundant expression. Nonetheless, I take this to refer to punishments and policies of control that make a point of being disproportionately harsh – as opposed to **retributive justice** (p67) that aims to give offenders the punishment they deserve.*

The perception that prisons are too comfortable and that punishment ought to be punitive is a common theme in Right Wing approaches to crime.

Punitive punishment is seen in the **'Short, Sharp Shock'** approach to punishing young offenders. This policy was introduced in 1979 by Margaret Thatcher's Conservative government. It reformed the old Borstals into Detention Centres for young offenders so that they would no longer be *"holiday camps"* but would instead provide a 3-month long military-style regime with early morning wake-up calls, lots of physical exercise and manual labour and only 30 minutes of conversation allowed between inmates each day.

Critics of the regimes pointed out that the old Borstals were pretty tough places and hardly 'holiday camps' but the regimes in the new DCs verged on torture. Reoffending rates did not change and the 'Short, Sharp Shock' regime was gradually mellowed, incorporating more opportunities for education and rehabilitation.

Punitive Control includes **Zero Tolerance Policing (ZTP)** which was pioneered in New York in the 1990s. This policy involves increasing the number of police officers on foot on the streets (as opposed to driving around in cars or in their offices) and instructing them to target minor crimes of disorder, such as jaywalking (crossing the road away from a pedestrian crossing, which is illegal in the USA), public drunkenness and urination, littering, graffiti and vandalism.

Within a few years of its introduction in New York, crime had dropped by 30-50% and New York went from being one of the world's most dangerous cities to being one of the safest. However, the period of ZTP in New York coincided with the **Great Crime Decline** (p24) and many other US cities experienced similar drops in crime despite not following the police.

ZTP is based on the **Broken Windows** theory (**Wilson & Kelling, 1982**). This **Right Realist** theory argues that people are influenced by disorder in their environment and are more likely to commit serious crimes if minor crimes seem to be being ignored.

Research: revisit your notes on **1A: Socialisation, Culture & Identity** you can link this to Wilson & Kelling and Broken Windows

AO2 ILLUSTRATION: ZERO TOLERANCE POLICING

ZTP became an official policy in New York under Right Wing Mayor **Rudy Giuliani** who was elected in 1993; during the 1990s the New York homicide rate fell by 82& compared to 53% in other cities. However, it had started falling before Giuliani was elected. **Bill Bratton**, the New York Police Chief, claims that ZTP was successful because it engaged with local communities and tackle the minor crimes that mattered to them, rather than coming down heavily on *all* crimes.

Bratton's analysis makes ZTP sound more like a version of **community crime prevention** *(p71).*

ZTP has been piloted in the UK in the 1990s, in the King's Cross area of London, Hartlepool, Middlesbrough and Strathclyde. It was championed by **Ray Mallon**, head of Middlesbrough CID, who promised to cut crime by 20% in 18 months using ZTP and achieved this – as he had cut crime by 38% in his previous post in Hartlepool. However, Mallon was suspended for misconduct.

Other than Mallon, ZTP has not been popular with British police forces. Critics claim it creates conflict with minority groups and leads to heavy-handed policing. One of the demands of the **Black Lives Matter** campaigns in 2020 was the end of ZTP in America.

RESEARCH PROFILE: PUNCH (2007)

Maurice Punch analyses attempt to import ZTP by police forces in the UK and the Netherlands.

Punch argues that ZTP under Bratton's leadership in New York really consisted of three different approaches: (**1**) **information-led policing** ("Compstat"), where officers met to analyse crime data and plan strategies; (**2**) "**Fixing Broken Windows**," which meant reclaiming parts of the city, building links with communities and involving business to reverse decline; (**3**) **assertive police presence** on the streets, targeting particular low-level crimes.

Punch contends that British and Dutch observers only adopted the third strategy of assertive policing, without noticing the importance of the other two.

Evaluating Right Wing Views on Crime Reduction

Right Wing views on crime reduction are immensely popular with the general public, who always want the government to 'get tough' on crime.

Situational and **environmental crime prevention** have been immensely successful and might explain much of the **Great Crime Decline** (p24). However, these developments are not really social policies. They are products of new technology that members of the public and businesses have taken advantage of. Remember that only 4% of CCTV cameras in the UK are run by the state? These developments are things that would have happened regardless of which government was in power, Right or Left Wing.

This sort of crime prevention and control also raises concerns, especially about **privacy**. New surveillance technology enables the state to 'snoop' on citizens as they go about their business and **civil liberties campaigners** argue this is a breach of human rights. Right Wing politicians tend to be in favour of privacy and oppose Big Government, so even though **automatic facial recognition technology** might prevent more crime if it were rolled out nationally (e.g. by detecting a wanted offender while they were walking their dog), Right Wingers will not always support it.

The other strand of Right Wing criminology involves getting tough on offenders. Despite **James Q Wilson**'s argument that what matters is preventing crime by making sure offenders know they will be caught, the focus always shifts to making punishments as harsh as possible. A key element in Right Wing thought is always that punishments are currently too soft and that the wrong people (convicted criminals, the **Underclass**, etc.) are having too easy a time.

Much research suggests that making punishments tougher tends to impact disproportionately on marginalised groups, who bear the brunt of heavy-handed policing and tough sentencing (and even the death penalty).

A good example of this is the way **Zero Tolerance Policing** is misrepresented as putting police on the streets and telling them to be aggressive. By itself, this only leads to a deterioration in police relations with communities and stirs up resentment. The other aspects of ZTP, such as **investing in declining neighbourhoods** and **information-led policing**, are not as exciting for the public and are, at the end of the day, policies that Left Wing politicians can support too.

The main criticism of Right Wing approaches is that, by focusing on the control of individual offenders, they neglect the wider social context of crime. They don't try to fix inequality or poverty or challenge discriminatory practices. They don't demand the police reform themselves. They assume that society is fine the way it is and the only motive behind doing crime is an evil nature. Left Wing approaches try to see the bigger picture.

On the other hand, Right Wing approaches do focus on the idea that crime is morally wrong and that it hurts people. The idea that offenders deserve punishment and morally need punishment is an important challenge to the Left Wing view that sees criminals as victims who don't need to change because society is really at fault.

SOCIAL/COMMUNITY CRIME PREVENTION & PUNISHMENT

These strategies are sometimes called an actuarial approach to crime. 'Actuarial' refers to the method used by insurance companies to work out risk, so an actuarial crime prevention strategy works out who is at risk of turning to crime and intervenes to prevent that before it happens. It is based on the idea that crime is not evenly distributed throughout society (c.f. **Farrington's Cambridge study** which identifies many risk factors for crime, p38).

Social crime prevention 'targets' particular people or groups for interventions, which could including parenting classes or pre-school lessons or family counselling. They are popular with Left Realists and Neo-Marxists because they address the **pre-crime circumstances** before a crime occurs.

Community crime prevention is an approach particularly associated with America that aims to divert young people from delinquencies by investing in youth clubs, extra lessons and mentoring systems to give at-risk children an older role model (e.g. **Big Brothers Big Sisters of America**).

One community programme that did cross from the USA to the UK in 1982 was the **Neighbourhood Watch** scheme, in which the police assist a street or estate in making their homes more secure, patrolling and reporting suspicious activity. NW schemes often collapse when residents feel the police do not respond to their reports; they work best in areas where residents are homeowners, married with children and over-40: in other words, well-off (source: **Bolton, 2006**).

In many ways, these approaches resemble **situational & environmental crime prevention** (p65), except they are trying to 'tweak' people's social circumstances rather than their physical surroundings.

As with those Right Wing preventative strategies, these are aimed at working class crime and not **white collar crime**. Marxists would argue that, even if these programmes produce improvements in people's living conditions, they don't do anything to tackle the **structural inequality** in in the Capitalist system (p75).

Community punishment is known as **community service** in the UK and was introduced in 1977. It is an alternative to a custodial (prison) sentence for offenders who commit less serious crimes (e.g. criminal damage, fraud, drugs). The court will order between 40-300 hours of community service, often removing graffiti, renovating damaged buildings, litter picking or decorating public places. Unemployed offenders do 3-4 days of service a week; those with jobs must schedule time in their evenings or weekends. **Ministry of Justice (2013)** figures suggest that 35% of offenders on community service reoffend within a year, but that is still 8% better than the reoffending rate for equivalent prison sentences.

One feature of these policies is that they are often endorsed by Right Wing politicians too, which makes you suspect there's nothing specifically Left Wing about them, except for increasing the involvement of the state in people's private lives (which is the only reason Right Wingers object to them).

AO2 ILLUSTRATION: THE TROUBLED FAMILIES PROGRAMME

The Troubled Families Programme (TFP) was set up in 2011 after the riots in British cities that year (pX). The Conservative-led government promised to 'turn around' 120,000 troubled families in order to reduce crime, truancy and other social problems. Families were considered to have 'turned around' if school attendance improved above 85%, youth crime reduced by 33% and anti-social behaviour reduced by 60%; alternatively, if a family member moved off benefits and into employment for 6 months.

The TFP claimed a 99% success rate, but a leaked independent evaluation suggested that it had not had any effect on criminality. Partly this was because the families targeted weren't particularly 'criminal' to begin with.

An interesting feature of the TFP is that you will see it described as a **Left Realist community programme** (it is based on the 'Respect agenda' set up by a previous Labour government) or as a **New Right** policy to get the **Underclass** back into work (p50). It could be seen as **both** of these things, which is a weakness of these policies from a specifically Left Wing viewpoint.

RESEARCH PROFILE: PARKS (1988)

The **Perry Preschool Project** is a famous research study started in 1962 by **David Weikart** in Michigan, USA. This community programme targeted 123 Black American children living in poverty and identified as at risk of educational failure, all age 3-4.

The children were divided randomly into two groups: 58 received the High/Scope pre-school programme from 1962-1967 and 65 children were assigned to a control group. The pre-school activity involved 2½ hour morning sessions in small groups (average child-teacher ratio 6:1). The activities involved decision making and problem solving. There was a weekly 1½ hour home visit to include the mother in the educational process.

According to a project bulletin by **Greg Parks (1999)**, by age 40, the group who received the programme had fewer arrests for violent crime, property crime or drugs; more had graduated from high school and found jobs. It is estimated that for every dollar spent on the programme, $17 was saved on welfare and prison costs.

*This is also an example of an unusual methodology in Sociology: a **longitudinal study** that is also a **field experiment**, comparing an experimental group with a control group.*

RESTORATIVE JUSTICE

Restorative Justice (RJ) brings together the offender and the people harmed by their crime, enabling everyone to play a part in repairing the harm and finding a way forward. In many ways it is the opposite of **retributive justice** (p67), since the focus is on fixing what was broken (including trust and self-estem) instead of making the offender suffer to the same degree as their victim.

The theory of RJ was introduced in **Howard Zehr**'s ground-breaking book *Changing Lenses* **(1990)** which credits the original practice of RJ to the Native Americans and the Maori of New Zealand before the arrival of European settlers. He defines the 'three pillars' of Restorative Justice as:

1. **Harms & Needs:** Who was harmed, what was the harm and how can it be repaired?
2. **Obligations:** Who is responsible how can they repair the harm?
3. **Engagement:** Victims and offenders have active roles in the process

RJ often involves a face-to-face meeting between the offender and the victim – or the victim's family. Alternatively there is indirect communication – for example, if the crime was sexual or violent. Shuttle mediation involves letter-writing or a video-taped message; a proxy is someone else who takes the place of one of the parties in the meeting and relates their responses.

RJ is often used as part of a reduced sentence for the offender or a requirement for a non-custodial sentence (such as doing community service and RJ instead of prison). Sometimes it is used *after* a prison sentence (**probation**) to rehabilitate the prisoner into society. It is always **voluntary**.

RJ is promoted by **Left Realists** (p56). It is based on the theory of the '**Square of Crime**' (**Matthews & Young, 1992**).

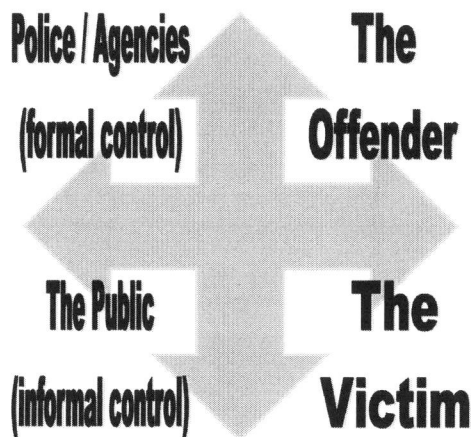

Police / Agencies
(formal control)

The
Offender

The Public
(informal control)

The
Victim

In this view, the interests of various groups intersect in a crime: the offender has harmed the victim and the victim needs redress or closure; the police/agencies have power over the offender (e.g. to punish) but public opinion shapes how this is done; the victim and the offender can appeal to the public (e.g. by appearing in the news media or just talking to friends and family).

In normal retributive justice, the police/agencies punish the offender, perhaps encouraged by public opinion, and the victim is side-lined. In RJ, the victim is put back into the equation and gets a say in how things are resolved.

John Braithwaite (1989) argues that retributive punishment causes **disintegrative shaming** – a sense of worthlessness that leads to reoffending. RJ leads to **integrative shaming**, which enables the offender to move on and re-join society. This is the opposite of the Right Wing view of **retribution leading to moral self-knowledge** (p67) and it assumes that offenders are genuine in their restorations (and not just saying what the victims and authorities expect of them).

AO2 ILLUSTRATION: FORGIVENESS FOR AMBER GUYGER

In 2018, off-duty (White) Dallas police office **Amber Guyger** shot and killed (Black) **Botham Jean**, believing he was an intruder (in fact she had walked into his apartment by mistake). She was convicted of murder. During the trial, **Brandt Jean**, the brother of the victim, gave announced he forgave Guyger and hugged her, asking her to "*give your life to Christ.*" The gesture was widely watched on TV.

This isn't an example of RJ, because it was a gesture in court inspired by Brandt Jean's Christian faith, rather than a planned meeting between the offender and the victim's family. However, Brandt Jean's mother said, "*Your load is lighter*" afterwards, which is the desired outcome for RJ.

There were criticisms of the gesture, with one online commentator posting: "*America should ask Black people forgiveness for serially asking African Americans to forgive sanctioned #PoliceBrutality.*" This illustrates a problem that RJ, by making the crime a private matter between victim and offender, can remove the need for **structural change in society** (p75).

Research: research real cases of RJ; watch the 2016 ITV documentary *Meeting My Enemy* about Jacob Dunne

RESEARCH PROFILE: SHERMAN & STRANG (2007)

Lawrence Sherman & Heather Strang carried out a review of good practice in RJ to determine its effectiveness. They gathered 424 research studies from an Internet search and reduced this to 34 studies from the UK, USA and Australia that provided an experimental comparison of a group experiencing RJ and a control group going through ordinary justice procedures.

The RJ groups showed a reduction in offending for violent and property offences; the victims showed reduced trauma and desire for revenge; they reported an increased ability to come to terms with what had happened. The researchers recommend RJ is more widely used in the UK.

The studies all involve small sample groups and come from different countries with different legal systems, making it hard to generalise the findings to the UK in all cases.

STRUCTURAL CHANGE IN SOCIETY

People who support Left Wing policies demand a structural change in society – not just tinkering with particular situations but changing the way society works for everyone. Left Wing criminology often focuses on the use of benefits to lift families out of poverty, reform of the police to change the way they interact with communities and challenging **institutional racism** in all areas of life.

Research: review your notes on **3A: Globalisation & the Digital Social World** and focus on Social Justice and the Anti-Globalisation Movement as examples of campaigning for structural change

Many Left Wing ideas are inspired by **Merton**'s insight that crime is caused by **structural strain** in society (p48). By reducing the strain (making society more equal), you reduce incentives for crime.

*Wait, isn't Merton a **Functionalist**? Yes, but **Strain Theory** influenced **Neo-Marxism** and **Left Realism**, who abandoned the Functionalist stuff about anomie but kept the focus on inequality*

For example, former chief constable Andy Cooke told **The Guardian** that if he had £5 billion to cut crime, he would put £1 billion into policing and £4 billion into reducing poverty: "*The best crime prevention is increased opportunity and reduced poverty*" (source: **Vikram Dodd, 2021**).

The **2018 Global Law & Order Report** suggests there is a correlation between equality and crime. 148,000 people in 142 countries completed a **victim survey** (p18) on whether they feel safe walking home alone and whether they trust the police. Countries were ranked according to how equally wealth is distributed there. In Venezuela, 80% do not feel safe walking home alone— kidnappings are common and it is the 19th most unequal in wealth. In Norway, 93% feel safe, but it is the 12th most equal country of the 142.

However, a correlation cannot prove cause-and-effect – and the country that comes out on top for safety is Singapore (94%) but Singapore is nowhere near the top for equality of wealth, so there must be other factors too.

A criticism of structural change is that it can just as easily **create** crime, since the outcomes are unpredictable. **Durkheim** (p6) argues that periods of rapid social change create **anomie**, even if those changes involve increasing equality.

For example, in 2001 the UK Labour government introduced **Working Family Tax Credits** (**WFTC**) to support low-paid families with children. The scheme was very popular and helped alleviate 'in-work poverty' and make working worthwhile (so it also addressed the New Right's criticism of benefit traps creating an **Underclass**, p50). However, it was blamed for driving up divorce, because a single mother could claim an extra £100 per week by splitting from her partner; in the three years after WFTC were introduced, the divorce rate among women with low-income husbands rose 160% (source: **Francesconi et al, 2009**). Right Wing critics argue that divorce contributes to delinquency and men without family responsibilities are more likely to be deviant.

Robert Merton termed this the *'law of unintended consequences'* – *when you interfere with a complex system, you cannot predict all the outcomes. It is often used by Right Wingers (e.g. James Q Wilson, p52) to justify sticking with the status quo*

AO2 ILLUSTRATION: CAPITAL HILL AUTONOMOUS ZONE (Chaz)

In 2020, the murder of a Black American named **George Floyd** by a police officer sparked worldwide protests under the banner of the **Black Lives Matter** movement (pX). Protestors in the Capital Hill area of Seattle formed an 'autonomous zone' (Chaz) where they banned the police from entering. They distributed free food and medical supplies and planted community gardens. One small group painted a large mural: *Black Lives Matter*.

Seattle's mayor Jenny Durkan said the zone could be the start of a "*summer of love.*" A visitor to Chaz described it to the BBC: "*There were classes, lectures, speakers, poetry, lots of live music, huge works of art... It was really beautiful.*"

The Chaz protestors demanded that funding for the police be cut by half and the money re-directed to health care and **restorative justice** (p73).

There were four shootings within the zone, two of which were fatal; allegations of sexual assaults emerged. Chaz supporters denied that these were carried out by the protesters. Nevertheless, on 1 July 2020, after 3 weeks of occupation, the police used force to clear the site (and reclaim their police station), with Seattle police chief Carmen Best declaring, "*Enough is enough.*"

If you are Left Wing, then Chaz indicates the possibility of a police-free society, which would be a huge structural change. If you are Right Wing, it illustrates the impossibility of such a utopia.

Research: find out more about Chaz and the other autonomous zones created by protestors in 2020; review your notes on **1A: Socialisation, Culture & Identity** and link this to Defunding The Police and formal agencies of social control

Welcome to Chaz (photo: Derek Simeone)

RESEARCH PROFILE: SULLIVAN & O'KEEFFE (2017)

In 2014 in New York, **Eric Garner** was killed while being arrested, triggering protests that ended with two police officers being fatally shot by an anti-police extremist. In response, New York Police Department (NYPD) conducted a **slowdown** for 7 weeks: they performed only essential duties and stopped issuing traffic tickets and using Stop & Search powers.

Christopher Sullivan & Zachary O'Keeffe analysed the **official crime statistics** during the slowdown. The arrest rate for serious crime (murder, rape, robbery, etc.) remained constant because these were still being policed normally. Minor crimes and drug offences dropped by 3-6%. This could be because the public didn't bother reporting crimes but the researchers identify the drop in crime lasting for a period after the slowdown finished. They suggest instead it was the *absence of police* that led to the reduction in crime.

The researchers suggest that the slowdown was *"a symbolic show of strength to demonstrate the city's dependence on the NYPD"* – but it seems to have demonstrated the opposite.

Sullivan & O'Keeffe conclude that proactive policing (when the police are on the streets looking for law-breaking to happen) actually *disrupts* communities and makes crimes more likely. This is a powerful argument against **Zero Tolerance Policing** (p68) and in favour of defunding the police.

However, it is based on an unusual period in New York City following a crisis of confidence in the NYPD and the results might not generalise to other cities and times. For example, in 2020 over 20 US cities (including New York) cut police budgets by a total of $840 million; however, the murder rate went up by 25% that year and America experienced a surge in violence. Critics debate whether this increase is due to reduced policing, the stresses of the 2020-21 Coronavirus Pandemic or other factors (like the possible end of the **Great Crime Decline**, p24).

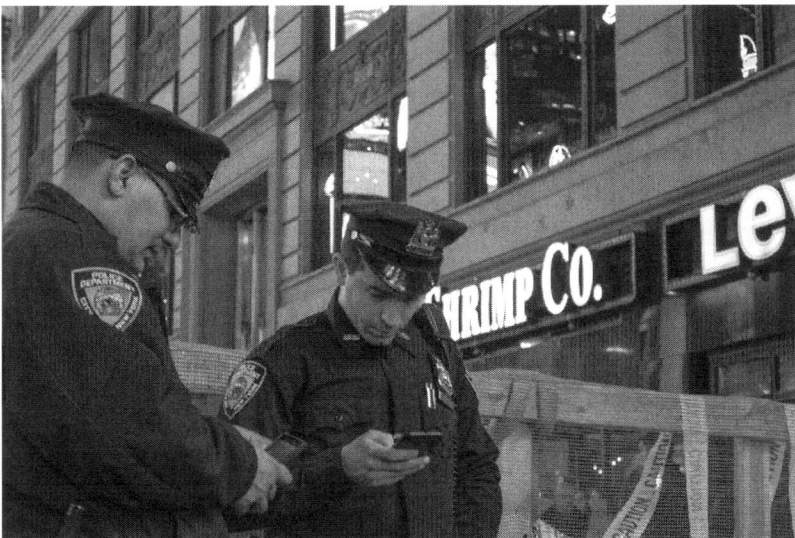

New York Police (photo: Matthias Kinsella)

Evaluating Left Wing Views on Crime Reduction

Left Wing views on crime reduction are less popular with the general public but have had more influence on social policy in the last 20 years.

Social and **community crime prevention** have been used by many governments and might explain much of the **Great Crime Decline** (p24). However, these policies are expensive. They are defended on the grounds that the money spent on them produces greater savings later (when future-criminals instead get jobs and pay taxes instead of going to prison and costing tax money). The law of unintended consequences means that these outcomes are never certain: training future-criminals in problem-solving might just make them more effective criminals, after all.

This sort of crime prevention and control also raises concerns, especially the role of Big Government in ordinary people's lives. Right Wingers claim that government meddling always backfires and regard the family as under threat (e.g. the controversy over the impact of Working Family Tax Credits).

The most interesting aspect of Left Wing criminology is **Restorative Justice** (**RJ**). This promises to be a new approach and one which is compatible with defunding the police and putting fewer people in prison. It also offers closure for victims who are often ignored (the Right Wing alternative, **retributive justice**, only reassures victims that the offender is suffering horribly). However, RJ only works if all parties volunteer for it and there are some crimes (e.g. rape) where being confronted by your abuser might *increase*, rather than reduce, the victim's trauma. It's possible to fake guilt and repentance and offenders who are **psychopaths** excel at this sort of deception and manipulation.

Moreover, reconciling victim and offender does nothing to fix structural problems in society and might even make them worse – such as insisting that Black victims of crime or police brutality ought to forgive their attacker rather than White people fixing the **institutional racism** in society. Of course, it's possible to do both and the **Square of Crime** reminds us that the public and the police/agencies are involved in every crime too.

Focusing on **structural changes in society** offers the hope of dealing with crime at the source: the inequality in society. The main criticism of this is that, by blaming society for crime and misbehaviour, Left Wingers neglect the offender's individual and personal responsibility. Crime is no longer seen as a moral problem that needs to be judged and condemned, but an economic or medical problem that needs to be cured.

On the other hand, Left Wing approaches do focus on the idea that crime is a **social construct** (p12) and that no one would choose to be a criminal and go to prison if they had better alternatives available to them. The job of Left Wing policies is to offer people those better choices. This often means challenging the assumption that we need heavy-handed policing or that there's nothing that can be done about poverty – or that it's a person's own fault that they are poor. Left Wing policies often claim to be motivated by compassion for the vulnerable people in society and that sometimes means compassion for criminals too.

EXAM PRACTICE: REDUCING CRIME & DEVIANCE

The OCR exam has three questions in **Paper 3 Section B**. Questions 7-9 are on Education and questions 10-12 are on Religion, Belief & Faith, but this Study Guide is focused on **Option 1** which covers questions **4-6**:

4. In what ways do crime prevention strategies reduce crime? **[10 marks: 6 AO1 + 4 AO2]**

This is one of those 'describe & illustrate' questions, but with no Source A or Source B to lean on. No need to evaluate.

*Choose two strategies to outline – you could choose Left Wing ones or Right Wing ones or one of each. It's a good idea to refer to named sociologists (like Clarke or Parks) and you should definitely use some sociological terminology (like structural inequality, rational choice). Then offer examples and make sure each example has an explanation of **why** it prevents crime. For example, "Target hardening includes steering locks on cars which makes it not worth the trouble for a rational criminal to break into a car."*

5. To what extent is restorative justice an effective strategy for reducing crime? **[20 marks: 8 AO1 + 4 AO2 + 8 AO3]**

This is a mid-size essay with a requirement for developed evaluation. You should spend 25 minutes and write at least 500 words.

*Write **three** points. Each point should introduce a sociological idea with some illustration from the real world. Each should finish off with a developed evaluation. For example, you could write about Zehr's three pillars, the Square of Crime and integrative shaming. Don't forget to offer a conclusion: will RJ actually work (Sherman & Strang is important for this)?*

6. Outline and evaluate Right Wing policies for reducing crime and deviance. **[40 marks: 16 AO1 + 8 AO2 + 16 AO3]**

This is the last of the two big (40 mark) essays in OCR A-Level Sociology. You should spend 50 minutes and write at least 1000 words.

*Write **five** points. Each point should introduce a sociological idea with illustration from the real world. Each should finish off with a developed evaluation. For example, you could write about target hardening, architectural policies, custodial sentences, the death penalty and Zero Tolerance Policing. The differing views of Functionalists, Right Realists and Marxists could all come into this as well as the question about whether Right Wing policies actually work (defunding the police is a useful issue to answer this).*

CHAPTER FIVE – EVALUATION

In **Paper 3 Section B (Option 1: Crime & Deviance)**, question 5 and 6 both assess **AO3**/evaluation and require a developed evaluation; this needs to address theoretical or methodological issues. It needs to go deeper than a 'brief evaluation' and look at an issue from alternative perspectives or work through the implications of a viewpoint.

As well as the evaluative points you can find in the preceding chapters, here are some evaluative positions candidates can adopt:

Brief Evaluations

These points are simple one that are hard to turn into developed points, so you might miss out on the higher AO3 band marks. Still, better to write something than nothing at all.

"Not all people…" / Over-generalising

Structuralist Perspectives (like **Functionalism** or traditional **Marxism** and **Feminism**) are particularly prone to sweeping generalisations. They often claim that everyone is motivated by the same thing or experiences the same oppression or wants the same outcomes. For example, Functionalists claim everyone shares the same basic values in society and Feminists claim all women are in some way oppressed.

To evaluate these ideas, point out that not all people fit into this mould. Not all unemployed people commit crimes, not all police are racist, not all criminals are deterred by the death penalty.

If you are writing about some empirical research, point out that its sample group doesn't resemble everyone. Not all delinquents are white like the ones that William Chambliss studied (p60).

It's important not to be formulaic. Say **why** not all people are like this: give an example of one of the exceptions. Not all criminals are deterred by the death penalty, because some people commit crimes **under the influence of drugs**. Not all delinquent teenagers are like Chambliss' schoolboys **because some are Black or Asian and they have their own problems with racism**.

"It's out-of-date…" / Time-locked

You will probably have noticed that an awful lot of sociological research comes from the 1950s, '60s and '70s. Those were important decades when a lot of ground-breaking Sociology was done. But do theories and samples from the 1970s tell us anything about the UK in the 21st century?

To evaluate these studies, point out that so much has changed. **Mass employment in factories has ended**, **equal rights for women** has arrived (at least, in principle), the UK has **become a multicultural societ**y, the **Internet** has transformed the way we communicate and find out about the world (this last point makes studies from the 1980s and early '90s out-of-date too).

Once again, it's important not to be formulaic. Say *why* one of these changes matters for this particular study: give an example of one of the exceptions. Holdaway's study of police occupational culture (p17) is out of date because *the Metropolitan Police has reformed itself after the Macpherson Report*. Chambliss' research into the Saints & Roughnecks (p60) is out-of-date *because in the 21st century, schools and towns have CCTV to catch kids truanting or misbehaving*.

"Nature rather than nurture…" / The Nature-Nurture Debate

Sociologists tend to assume that everything is socially constructed, but it's worth remembering that biology might be playing a neglected role in human behaviour.

To evaluate these ideas, point out that a Nativist approach might be better. Rather than explain crime through social control, maybe there are innate biological processes that go on in criminals.

It would be formulaic just to say "maybe there are innate biological changes" and leave it at that. Say *why* the Nativist approach would be better: give an example of one of the benefits. Take a Nativist approach to studying crime, *because it might tell you the role testosterone places in male crime in lots of different cultures*.

Developing Evaluations

These points are suitable for Q5 or Q6. Their complexity makes them suitable for turning into developed points, so you can qualify for higher AO3 band marks.

"It's a macro-perspective / Interactionist critique

Structuralist Perspectives make sweeping generalisations because they study society as a whole and focus on important institutions rather than individual people. The **Interactionist** Perspective criticises this, saying it is better to look at society 'from the bottom up' (a **micro Perspective**). The sociologist Max Weber recommends using *Verstehen* – empathic understanding – rather than focusing on big trends.

To evaluate these ideas, point out that an Interactionist approach might be better. Rather than studying the Underclass as a trend in society, take a micro approach and study individual members of the Underclass.

Avoid being formulaic. Say **why** the micro approach would be better: give an example of one of the benefits. Take a micro approach to studying the Underclass, ***because they will tell you why they are unemployed, which may or may not have anything to do with a benefits trap***.

Development

If you bring in Interactionism as the solution to the problem, don't stop there. You could give examples of studies that employ this micro approach (like **Chambliss** studying delinquents, p60) or explain how later research incorporates aspects of the micro approach (like the way Left Realism involves the **Square of Crime**, p73).

Alternatively, criticise your own improvement: discuss the drawbacks of using the micro approach (the Underclass people might lie to the interviewer; after all, they are supposed to have no sense of right and wrong according to **Murray**, p51).

"This is similar to..." / Comparisons

Sometimes, different sociologists or different Perspectives end up saying similar things, although usually for different reasons Marxists and Feminists both agree there is propaganda and brainwashing (**ideology**) in the news. Marxists and Functionalists both agree that modern Capitalism is stressful and difficult for the poor. Interactionists and Marxists both agree that the police label people.

To evaluate these ideas, point out the similarity between the sociology you are writing about and another Perspective or research study. If you have explained that Marxists think that there is selective policing, explain that Interactionists also think that labels create a moral panic about 'folk devils' (p29).

As usual, don't be formulaic. Say **why** the two approaches are so similar **or** say why they are also different: give an example. Marxists and Interactionist agree on policing because they both think that crime is socially constructed, ***although Marxists think this comes from serving the ruling class*** and ***Interactionists focus more on how moral panics lead to deviancy amplification spirals***.

Development

If you think two Perspectives are similar, don't stop there. You could give examples of studies from each perspective, like **Hall**'s study of moral panics about Black muggers (p27) compared to **Cohen**'s study of Mods & Rockers (p29); or explain how later research incorporates both perspectives, like the Neo-Marxists of ***The New Criminology*** using Interactionist techniques.

Alternatively, criticise the very similarity you suggested: discuss the how differences between the two approaches are more important than similarities (Marxists recognise the overall social context of Capitalism, whereas Interactionists look at each social situation separately and miss out on the big picture).

"A Left/Right Winger would say …" / Political critique

Research into crime and deviance has a practical application: politicians use these ideas to pass laws and to launch or abolish social policies. Some of these are successful, others backfire. It's a good idea to praise sociological research if it leads to effective social policies or criticise it if it doesn't.

In order to avoid being formulaic, say *why* the research has practical benefits or drawbacks: give an example. Victim surveys support Left Wing approaches to crime prevention, *because they give the victim's perspective, which is important for Restorative Justice.*

Development

If you think a political implication is good or bad, don't stop there. You could give examples of studies which back up this political position, such as **Sherman & Strang**'s recommendations that RJ is widely used in the UK (p74).

Alternatively, criticise the political idea you suggested: discuss the flaws with focusing too much on victims (such as the way it can distract Left Wingers from working towards **structural change in society**).

"A weakness of this Perspective is …" / Standard theoretical critiques

Functionalism

Functionalism ignores diversity: Functionalism assumes we are all the same and want the same things, but the things it says we all want tend to be the sort of things that the white middle classes want. Functionalism doesn't take seriously the idea that ethnic minorities, the working class or women might have different goals and values.

Functionalism ignores social injustice: Functionalism assumes that society is harmonious and **meritocratic** but it turns a blind eye to a lot of inequality, corruption and barriers to social mobility. It defends Capitalism as the best system we have discovered for making people healthy and wealthy while ignoring the huge human and environmental cost of Capitalism worldwide. It is also prepared to accept a lot of crime for the sake of consensus.

Functionalism celebrates Western superiority: Functionalists believe in the **'March of Progress'** and claim that the sort of liberal democratic nations you find in Europe, North America and Australia are the most advanced. Other societies ought to imitate them and immigrants ought to fit in. This ignores many flaws in Western societies (e.g. Capitalism, patriarchy, institutional racism).

Functionalism overrates the biological: Functionalists believe society reflects unchangeable biological needs or 'human nature.' Critics argue there is no such thing as 'human nature' and that everything is **socially constructed**. 'Human nature' is often used to excuse certain crimes (such as male violence, prostitution or rape).

Development

If you offer a theoretical weakness, don't stop there. You could give examples of studies that illustrate that weakness (like Falk's study that suggests a small number of people commit most of the serious crime). Alternatively, follow through the implications of this weakness (what would happen if Right Wing politicians acted on Functionalist ideas) or bring in other Perspectives that have something to say about this weakness (like Marxists characterising Functionalist ideas as serving hegemonic power).

Alternatively, criticise the weakness you suggested by arguing that it isn't really a weakness: like James Q Wilson's idea that the factors involved in making a more equal society are beyond anyone's control so it's better to focus on what can be controlled and change the physical environment to reduce crime.

Make a point of discussing how Subcultural Theory improves on the standard Functionalist position in various ways – but at the cost of abandoning certain important Functionalist ideas. You can discuss how Right Realism improves on Functionalism in the same way.

The New Right

The New Right lacks empirical support: Most of the support for the New Right comes from news stories about working class deviance – but those stories might be exaggerated. Hard evidence for the existence of an **underclass** is not plentiful and there's even less evidence for a whole group of people (rather than a few individuals) who reject society's values, don't want to work, don't want to live in families and embrace crime as a lifestyle.

The New Right demonises the vulnerable: The New Right is accused of 'punching down' – targeting the group in society that most needs help and making them out to be monstrous and calling for any sort of help (in the form of benefits) to be taken away. **Marxists** find it fairly easy to characterise the New Right as a **hegemonic attack on the poor**. However, Marxists can be characterised as glamorising delinquents and criminals as noble underdogs and ignoring the damage they do in society.

The New Right exaggerates deviancy: The New Right presents the underclass as a growing problem that threatens the whole of society. Even **Functionalists** criticise this approach as alarmist. Functionalists believe that deviancy is necessary and ultimately benefits society. However, the New Right emerged partly because both Functionalists and Marxists seemed to be making excuses for crime rather than doing anything practical to put a stop to it.

Development

If you offer a theoretical weakness, don't stop there. You could give examples of studies that illustrate that weakness (like Murray's warning that single mothers are raising feral boys and promiscuous girls illustrates the New Right demonising the vulnerable). Alternatively, follow through the implications of this weakness (what would happen if politicians acted on Murray's suggestions) or bring in other Perspectives that have something to say about this weakness (like Marxists characterising the attack as serving hegemonic power).

Alternatively, criticise the weakness you suggested by arguing that it isn't really a weakness: Murray thinks the real enemies of the poor are the people who keep them in a benefits trap that appears kind but is actually dehumanising – you would be doing the underclass a favour by getting them off benefits and into family arrangements.

Make a point of discussing how Right Realism improves on the standard New Right position in various ways – but at the cost of abandoning certain important New Right ideas.

Marxism

Marxism ignores progress: In the last 200 years, Capitalist societies have abolished slavery, set up human rights, created a welfare state and free education and healthcare for all. Marxists often talk as if this hasn't happened or as if it happened *in spite of* Capitalism. This pessimistic view of the past and the future perhaps exaggerates social injustice as much as Functionalism downplays it.

Marxism is a conspiracy theory: It's standard for Marxists to argue that the Media (especially the news), Education and the Workplace are all controlled by a sinister group of billionaires who brainwash everyone through **ideology**. This underestimates the independence of many journalists, politicians and police officers well as the ability of ordinary people to think for themselves and work out what's true.

Marxists assume class is homogenous: *Homogenous* means 'all the same' and traditional Marxists think that all working class people share the same relationship to labour and power. However, **Neo-Marxists** are more aware of **intersecting Identities** and how behaviour is shaped by the particular circumstances.

Marxism offers no solutions: You don't have to be a Marxist to spot the Capitalism has flaws – Functionalists would admit *that*! Marxists argue that Capitalism is intrinsically rotten and destructive and it needs to be replaced rather than reformed. But replaced with what? Marxism can be accused of criticising Capitalism without offering a coherent alternative. Similarly, it identifies Youth Deviance as resistance, but doesn't suggest what can be done about its destructive aspects.

Development

If you offer a theoretical weakness, develop them. You could give examples of studies that illustrate that weakness (like Sullivan & O'Keeffe suggesting the police could be defunded without saying what should be put in its place). Alternatively, follow through the implications of this weakness (what would happen if Left Wing politicians acted on Marxist suggestions) or bring in other Perspectives that have something to say about this weakness (like Functionalists characterising Marxism as ignoring the impact of crimes on victims).

Alternatively, criticise the weakness you suggested by arguing that it isn't really a weakness: Marxism might sometimes look like a conspiracy theory but the big newspapers, Right Wing politicians and police chiefs could all be 'on the same side' without deliberately conspiring so long as they share vested interests.

Make a point of discussing how Neo-Marxism improves on the standard Marxist position in various ways – but at the cost of abandoning certain important Marxist ideas. You can discuss how Left Realism improves on Neo-Marxism in the same way.

Feminism

Feminism ignores biology: Feminists insist that gender is **socially constructed,** and it certainly is up to a point. However, Psychology reveals lots of biological differences in brain structure, hormones and genes between the sexes and it's unlikely that *none* of this makes *any* difference to social behaviour. But if Gender Identity is even partly based on unchangeable sexual differences, then some of the situations women are in might not be *entirely* due to Patriarchy.

Feminism ignores progress: In the last century women have won the vote, the right to be educated at university and manage their own affairs. In Britain, the Sexual Discrimination Act (1975) has outlawed sexual discrimination. Feminism can be accused of downplaying this progress and exaggerating the scale of injustice. However, the Sarah Everard murder can be used to show that women in the 21st century are still not safe.

Feminists assume gender is homogenous: As with Marxists and social class, traditional Feminists are accused of treating all women as if they experienced the same oppression – which in practice means assuming that the difficulties of White women are typical for all women. Clearly, young women (and especially young lesbian women) have different experiences.

Feminists ignore the oppression of men: Feminists sometimes seem to assume that Masculinity is homogenous and all men are complicit in the Patriarchy, but men are much more likely than women to die by violence, to be victims of crime and to work in dangerous conditions. Many young men are also victims of oppression and die in dangerous jobs, through violence or suicide.

Development

If you offer a theoretical weakness, develop it. You could give examples of studies that illustrate that weakness (like Adler arguing that progress in women's liberation has encouraged female crime while ignoring testosterone in male crime). Alternatively, follow through the implications of this weakness (what would happen if Left Wing politicians acted on Feminist suggestions, such as the 'curfew on men') or bring in other Perspectives that have something to say about this weakness (like Marxists agreeing that Capitalism oppresses men and women in different ways).

Alternatively, criticise the weakness you suggested by arguing that it isn't really a weakness: Feminism might ignore progress but the murder of Sarah Everard shows that women are still being murdered by men and the police who are supposed to protect them do not do so.

You could discuss how 4th Wave Feminism improves on the standard Feminist position in various ways – but at the cost of abandoning certain important Feminist ideas.

Interactionism

Interactionism cannot be generalised: Because it tends to do research on small groups, studying micro relationships and beliefs, it's hard to generalise the conclusions of Interactionism to other groups or society on a macro level.

Interactionists cannot be objective: The close-up and personal nature of Interactionist research and its focus on *Verstehen* makes it very **subjective** – just a matter of opinion – whereas Sociology claims to be a social *science* that explores facts in an **objective** way.

Interactionism is an incomplete explanation: Even when Interaction identifies processes that seem to be quite generalisable – like the **Self-Fulfilling Prophecy** – its small-scale micro view means it doesn't explore where these processes come from. Marxists argue that Interactionism is incomplete as an explanation without including Capitalism and **ruling class ideology**. Functionalists would also say Interactionism needs to explain how the experiences of little groups fit into a theory of society's functions and requirements.

Development

If you offer a theoretical weakness, develop them. You could give examples of studies that illustrate that weakness (like Chambliss' study being limited to Seattle teenagers or Cohen to the 1960s). Alternatively, follow through the implications of this weakness (what would happen if politicians acted on Interactionist suggestions) or bring in other Perspectives that have something to say about this weakness (like Neo-Marxism claiming to offer an explanation of where labels come from in the first place).

Alternatively, criticise the weakness you suggested by arguing that it isn't really a weakness: Interactionism might lack objectivity but the point about *verstehen* is that it gives insight into what 'makes people tick' rather than focusing on statistics or mass trends.

You could discuss how Neo-Marxism and Left Realism improve on the standard Interactionist position in various ways – but perhaps at the cost of abandoning the micro perspective in Interactionism.

EXAM PRACTICE: SECTION B

The OCR exam has three questions in **Paper 3 Section B**. Questions 7-9 are on Education and questions 10-12 are on Religion, Belief & Faith, but this Study Guide is focused on **Option 1** which covers questions **4-6**:

4. In what ways is victimisation distributed differently by age? **[10 marks: 6 AO1 + 4 AO2]**

This is one of those 'describe & illustrate' questions, but with no Source A or Source B to lean on. No need to evaluate.

*Choose two points to outline – you could choose the young and the elderly. It's a good idea to refer to named sociologists (like Farrington) and you should definitely use some sociological terminology (like life course, fear of crime vs vulnerability to crime). Then offer examples and make sure each example has an explanation of **why** it involves victimisation of an age group. For example, "Elderly people are less at risk of crime because they don't go out to unfamiliar or dangerous places as much as the young but 8 out of 10 doorstep scams are carried out on the elderly."*

5. To what extent is the New Right an effective explanation for crime and deviance? **[20 marks: 8 AO1 + 4 AO2 + 8 AO3]**

This is a mid-size essay with a requirement for developed evaluation. You should spend 25 minutes and write at least 500 words.

*Write **three** points. Each point should introduce a sociological idea with some illustration from the real world. Each should finish off with a developed evaluation. For example, you could write about worklessness, illegitimate births and Murray's idea of the benefits trap. Don't forget to offer a conclusion: does the New Right actually explain anything?*

6. Outline and evaluate Left Wing policies for reducing crime and deviance. **[40 marks: 16 AO1 + 8 AO2 + 16 AO3]**

This is the last of the two big (40 mark) essays in OCR A-Level Sociology. You should spend 50 minutes and write at least 1000 words.

*Write **five** points. Each point should introduce a sociological idea with illustration from the real world. Each should finish off with a developed evaluation. For example, you could write about social crime prevention, community service, restorative justice, reducing inequality and defunding the police. The differing views of Marxists, Neo-Marxists and Left Realists could all come into this as well as the question about whether Left Wing policies actually work (examples like Chaz and WFTC could help with this).*

KEY RESEARCH

The 31 studies here cover all the topics that arise in this Section of the exam and they will prove just as useful in later sections too. Start learning them. For each study, I include the key terms, a Perspective (if relevant) and the particular topics it is linked to.

Adler (1975): *Sisters In Crime*, Liberation Thesis, female criminality; **Feminist**; social construction, relativism, patterns of gender, p33

Bates (2014): *Everyday Sexism*, **Feminist**; social construction, relativism, patterns of gender, p28

Beck (1992): *The Risk Society*, late modernity, risk, transgressive criminology; **Interactionist**; green crime, p42

Beckett & Evans (2018): capital punishment, implicit bias; **Left Realist**; social construction, relativism, patterns of ethnicity, retributive justice, p68

Chambliss (1973): *The Saints & the Roughnecks*, labelling; **Interactionist, Neo-Marxist**; Interactionist/Neo-Marxist explanations, p60

Cloward & Ohlin (1960): legitimate & illegitimate opportunity structures, criminal, conflict, retreatist; **Functionalist**; Subcultural explanation, p49

Cohen, S (1972): *Folk Devils & Moral Panics*, 1964 Mods v Rockers riots; **Interactionism**; media & deviance, p29

Falk et al. (2013): Swedish study, chronic offenders; **Functionalist**; patterns & trends, p26

Farrington et al. (2006): *Cambridge Study*, longitudinal, chronic offenders; **Interactionist**; self-report study, patterns of age, p38

Fitzgerald et al. (2002): *Policing For London*, institutional racism; **Left Realist**; social construction, relativism, patterns of ethnicity, p35

Glenny (2008): *McMafia*, McDonalisation of crime, Bulgarian Mafia; organised global crime, p40

Gordon (1971): *Class & the Economics of Crime*, selective policing; **Neo-Marxist**; Marxist explanations, p54

Hall (1978): *Policing the Crisis*, moral panic over Black muggers; **Neo-Marxist**; subculture & ethnicity, deviant delinquent subcultures, media & deviance, p27

Holdaway (1980): police occupational culture, police discretion, selective policing; **Neo-Marxist**; patterns of class, social construction, p17

Jones (2011): *Chavs*, stigma, moral panic; **Neo-Marxist**; social construction, relativism, patterns of class, p31

Jones, Maclean & Young (1986): Islington Crime Survey; **New Right**; patterns of class & gender, victim survey, p19

Lea & Young (1984): *What's To Be Done About Law & Order?*, relative deprivation, marginalisation, subculture; **Left Realist**; Left Realist explanations, p56

Merton (1938): Strain Theory, anomie, innovation; **Functionalism**; Functionalist explanation, p48

Mumsnet (2012): Sexual Assault Survey; **Feminist**; victim survey, patterns of gender, p15

Murray (1984): underclass; **New Right**; New Right explanation, patterns of class, p51

Newman (1972): *Defensible Space*, architecture; **Functionalist**; environmental crime prevention, p66

Parks (1988): Perry Preschool Project; **Left Realist**; community crime prevention, patterns of age, p72

Pearson (1983): *Hooligans*, Teddy boys; **Neo-Marxist**; social construction, relativism, patterns of age, p14

Punch (2007): Zero Tolerance Policing; **Right Realist**; punitive control, p69

Sharkey (2018): *Uneasy Peace*, Great Crime Decline; **Left Realist**; patterns & trends, social policies, p25

Shaw (1930): *The Jack Roller*; **Interactionist**; self-report studies, patterns of age, p22

Sherman & Strang (2007): restorative justice; **Left Realist**; restorative justice, p74

Smart (1976): *Women, Crime & Criminology*, strict socialisation, doubly deviant; **Feminist**; Feminist explanations, patterns of gender, p59

Sullivan & O'Keeffe (2017): NYPD slowdown, Zero Tolerance Policing; **Left Realist**; structural change, punitive control, p77

Taylor, Walton & Young (1972): *The New Criminology*, critical criminology, fully social theory; **Neo-Marxist**; Radical Criminology explanations, p55

Wilson (1975): *Thinking About Crime*, social order, rational choice; **Neo-Marxist**; Right Realist explanations, p52

FURTHER RESEARCH

These studies are less central to any argument. Some of them just reference a useful piece of terminology. Others offer criticism of a Key Study or are the original research that a Key Study is criticising.

Alexander (1997): sex work is liberating, p33

Becker (1963): *Outsiders*, labelling theory, p13

Bindel (2017): sex work is rape, p58

Bourgois (1995): relative deprivation, p22

Box (1983): selective policing, p21

Braithwaite (1989): supports restorative justice, p74

Campbell (1981): self-reports show no gender divide, p21

Clarke (1983): crime prevention, p65

Cohen (1955): status frustration, p49

Cornish & Clarke (1986): rational choice theory, p51

Durkheim (1883): social solidarity, p6

Durkheim (1895): society of saints, p12

Estrada et al. (20015): male crime patterns resembling women's, p33

Farrell (2007): CSEW underestimates crime, p19

Francesconi et al. (2009): criticises WFTC, p75

Garfunkel (1956): criticises retributive justice, p67

Heidensohn (1985): criticises Chivalry Thesis, p58

Hobbs & Dunningham (1998): glocalised organised crime, p39

Hollin (1989): Dark Figure of unrecorded crime, p15

Lambert (1970): police discretion, p17

Lemert (1967): secondary deviance, p59

Hanley (2011): criticises **Jones (2011)**, p31

Jackson (2006): 'laddish' girls, p33

Marx (1858): base and superstructure, p6

Matthews & Young (1992): the Square of Crime, p73

Parsons (1951): functional prerequisites valve, p9

Pearson & Rowe (2020): bias in Stop & Search, p34

Phillips (1999): criticises **Murray (1984)**, p51

South (2008): primary vs secondary green crime, p40

Snodgrass (1972): followed up **Shaw (1930)**, p22

Thompson et al. (2012): crime peaks in 2003, p25

Valenti (2011): supports SlutWalks, p14

Walklate (1995): criticises Chivalry Thesis, p58

Weber (1905): invention of Capitalism, p10

Weber (1922): social actions, p7

White (2008): anthropocentric vs ecocentric harm, p41

Young (1984): social bulimia, p53

Young (2003): criticises New Right, p50

Zehr (2003): *Changing Lenses*, restorative justice, p73

GLOSSARY

Anomie: literally means "without norms" and it refers to the sense of disconnection and anxiety that occurs when people do not feel a connection to their society and their work; Functionalists say it is caused by the breakdown of **social solidity** and a lack of **value consensus**

Capitalism: an economic system that promotes the private ownership of property, the pursuit of profit and the concentration of wealth in the hands of a minority of people; the opposite is Communism, which abolishes private property to make everyone economically equal

Crime: an act that breaks the laws of the state, bringing formal sanctions on the criminal

Culture: the set of norms and values passed on by one generation to the next, including a version of history and traditional institutions that make up a way of life; cultures vary from one society to another and change (slowly) over time

Deterrence: the effect of making people law-abiding by showing them the negative consequences of crime for themselves

Deviance: Behaviour that goes against **norms** and **values**

Deviancy Amplification Spiral: a process where a deviant **label** is acted upon by the authorities, leading to harsh sanctions and increased attention paid to the **deviancy**, exaggerating the **moral panic**

Feminism: a sociological Perspective that identified conflict between the sexes; believes in a Patriarchy which subordinates women and maintains male power through coercion and violence

Folk Devil: a group identified as a threat to society during a **moral panic**

Functionalism: a sociological Perspective that promotes consensus around shared values; believes in a biological basis for human social behaviour and the inevitability of deviance

Gender: the norms and values linked to biological sex; males are often expected to behave in a masculine way and females in a feminine way: male/female are sexes but masculine/feminine are genders

Globalisation: a process going on that makes different parts of the world more interconnected through travel, global **Capitalism** and the **Mass Media**

Hegemony: the dominance of one group and their culture in society; hegemonic culture is the version of culture that commands the most respect; according to **Neo-Marxists** hegemonic culture manufactures consent

Ideology: a set of ideas and values that influence how people interpret society; ideology is usually promoted by the **hegemonic** culture hides and justifies things which go against that culture; for example, a racist ideology might make people ignore racism or (if they can't ignore it) view racism as justified

Institutional Racism: a form of systemic bias that makes people within an institution carry out racist practices even though they may not personally harbour racist views

Interactionism: a sociological Perspective that adopts a micro (small scale) approach; believes in understand individual motives and perceptions, often through examining how people play social roles or internalise **labels**

Intersectionality: A 21st century approach to Sociology which focuses on how different identities combine to create privilege or oppression

Labelling Theory: an **Interactionist** explanation of deviance due to social labels with master status that are internalised, producing a self-fulfilling prophecy, according to **Becker (1963)**

Latent function: The hidden effects of social institutions, that befit society without us noticing

Left Wing: a political tendency to value progress, equality and justice highly

Manifest function: The obvious effects of social institutions, that benefit society in ways we all recognise

Marxism: a sociological Perspective that identifies conflict between social classes; believes in a **ruling class** exploiting a **working class**, both through violet force and **ruling class ideology**

Mass Media: technological forms of communication that can reach millions (or billions of people); traditionally radio, TV, film and print but now including the digital media, such as websites, social media, text messaging and mobile phones

Meritocracy: A system that rewards talent and effort with social advancement; specifically, the idea that education recognises and gives qualifications to the most intelligent people, assigning them to the most important jobs with the biggest rewards. The opposite is **social reproduction**.

Moral Panic: process where the Media identifies a group as a threat, exaggerates its importance, arouses public concern and brings about new policies and social change

Neo-Marxism: several new interpretations of **Marxism** that emerged in the 1970s and became mainstream in the 1990s, incorporating elements of **Interactionism** to Marxist thought

New Right: a sociological Perspective that proposes we are experience social collapse brought on by a welfare culture that rewards worklessness and deviance in the **Underclass**

Norms: ways of behaving seen as acceptable or expected in society; based on underlying **values**

Patriarchy: The way society is structured around the interests of males, giving status to masculine behaviour and values and systematically subordinating women; masculine **hegemony** in society

Postmodernism: a sociological Perspective that proposes we are living in a new phase of social development, characterised by media saturation, diversity, choice, fluidity and fragmentation

Right Wing: a political tendency to value privacy, freedom and family values highly

Ruling class: A **hegemonic** group in society that controls the wealth and power, supported by an ideology that either hides or justifies their influence; Marx termed the ruling class 'the bourgeoisie' but **Neo-Marxists** often term it the **Hegemony**

Ruling class ideology: a set of beliefs promoted by the ruling class to preserve their power over the working class; ideology hides the injustice in society and justifies it when it cannot hide it

Social class: A system for separating people based on their economic position (wealth, income, status); originally a split between the **ruling class** and **working class**, but later admitting of a middle class in between and now many more classes

Socialisation: The process of acquiring norms and values due to upbringing (primary socialisation) and education/experience (secondary socialisation)

Social reproduction: the opposite of **Meritocracy**; the idea that social divisions are reproduced each generation despite the education people receive

Social solidarity: The experience of 'belonging' in society, linked to **value consensus**; it is the opposite of **anomie**

Subculture: a group within society that shares some of the **norms and values** of mainstream society but also has distinctive norms and values of its own

Transgression: Behaviour that goes against the rules or laws; similar to **deviance**

Underclass: term used by the **New Right** for a class below the working class, characterised by single mothers on benefits, poorly socialised children and irresponsible, workless and crime-prone adult males

Value consensus: The set of norms and values around which there is (supposedly) broad agreement in society; includes views on history, religion, morality, lifestyle and wealth

Values: powerful ideas shared by people in a culture about what is right and desirable and what is shameful or wrong; often expressed in behaviour as **norms**

Western culture: the culture of the UK, European countries, North America and Australia, that emerged out of the shared experience of Christianity, the Industrial Revolution and the development of democracy; an important part of **Global Culture**; responsible for developing Capitalism

White collar crime: crime carried out by powerful people in the course of doing their respectable jobs; includes embezzling money, tax fraud, breaking health & safety regulations and environmental pollution.

Working class: The majority group in society that is systematically excluded from access to wealth and power; controlled by **ideology** and the threat of force by the **ruling class**; Marx terms the working class 'the proletariat.'

ABOUT THE AUTHOR

Jonathan Rowe is a teacher of Religious Studies, Psychology and Sociology at Spalding Grammar School and he creates and maintains **www.psychologywizard.net** and the **www.philosophydungeon.weebly.com** site for Edexcel A-Level Religious Studies. He has worked as an examiner for various Exam Boards but is not affiliated with OCR. This series of books grew out of the resources he created for his students. Jonathan also writes novels and creates resources for his hobby of fantasy wargaming. He likes warm beer and smooth jazz.

Printed in Great Britain
by Amazon